Ninja Communications:
The Art and Science of Influence

Oscar Hines

USA

Copyright © 2017 by **Oscar Hines**

All rights reserved. No part of this publication may be reproduced, distributed or transmitted in any form or by any means, without prior written permission.

Oscar Hines
Genuine Journey LLC
397 North Sam Houston Parkway East
Suite 110
Houston, TX 77060
www.oscarhines.com

Ninja Communications: The Art and Science of Influence/ Oscar Hines. --
1st print ed.
ISBN 978-0-9996400-2-9

I dedicate this book to my four beautiful children, Mercedes, Austin, Brooke and Miles. Without knowing it, they saved me from myself. They taught me how to love unconditionally, sacrifice relentlessly, face my fears, lead by example and laugh at myself when I wanted to take myself too seriously.

Each of these wonderful beings are great communicators, but most importantly are each other's best friends. I am proud to be their parent, mentor, and friend. To them and others I say, embrace this amazing Journey we call life. See what you want to create, rehearse it in your mind and materialize it. When you are afraid, be still, trust your creator and trust yourself, then take decisive action and push past the fear. When you find your passion, that which you were intended to do on this planet, pursue it with all the energy it deserves! Celebrate life, and at the end of this journey, you will be Celebrated.

CONTENTS

Foreword by Mr. Les Brown 7
Preface: How to Get the Most from this Book 10
Holistic Communications 25
The Many Facets of Communication 35
Listening, an Active Process 56
Becoming a Ninja Master in The Art of Communication 64
Emotions and the Cause-And-Effect on our Bodies 103
The Science and Mystery of Energy 115
Public Speaking 127
Effective Leaders Get Results 136
Importance of Communication in Building Relationships .. 171
Men, Women and the Chemistry of Attraction 177
A New Way to View the Experience of Communication 185
References 188
About the Author 190

• FOREWORD •

Foreword by Les Brown

VICTOR FRANKEL SAID, "Don't ask what is the meaning of life, ask what is the meaning of your life." Oscar Hines, entrepreneur, radio talk show host, dynamic speaker and author, has written a book that is designed to assist you in living a purposeful life. **Ninja Communications: The Art and Science of Influence** will take you through a step by step, proven process that will empower you to create collaborative, achievement-driven relationships, and more.

Speaker George Fraser said, "Your network determines your net worth." I admire the depth of thinking and unique approach Oscar brings to this highly talked about topic. You might ask 'what makes this book stand out from all the rest?' After coming to this country at a very young age, Oscar didn't speak the language, but those who knew him quickly became aware that he was determined to become successful and he had an insatiable curiosity for words, and how they affected people. He once challenged his college professor by answering a question in a way that only Oscar would, his answer had the professor and all the students scratching their heads asking, 'where did that come from?'

To become influential, you must learn to discipline your tongue, become a deep listener, and commit yourself to getting to know people by asking questions and observing behavior which can reveal a great deal about them.

Oscar is a people watcher from back in the day. He believes people watching is required to gain the insight necessary to transform minds, touch hearts, and give people hope. Oscar's changing lives with this book and by providing inspirational programming daily on his Houston-based radio station, **Synergy Radio**, which is rapidly expanding across the country. People are loving it!

I have partnered with Oscar to help people become motivated and hungry to live a larger life. Over the years I've heard people say practice what you preach, Oscar preaches what he has practiced. This book raises the bar on the conversation about influence! I've learned so much by reading and applying these principles of influence and it has literally changed my life as I am sure it will yours. As T.D. Jakes would say, "Get Ready, Get Ready, Get Ready to soar to new heights." Ninja Communications the Art and Science of Influence is a game changer. Oscar knows a thing or two because he has seen a thing or two.

This book will positively impact your personal, family, and financial life. I love it! You have Greatness in You, Ninja Communications the Art and Science of Influence will bring out that Greatness, from my lips to God's ears, enjoy.

Les Brown

• PREFACE •

How to Get the Most from this Book

WHEN GETTING INTO THE SUBJECT of communication it can be vastly complex because it takes on different aspects of our interactions, from personal to business. As you read this book; you will find that some things you already knew and others will be completely new to you. The first few chapters cover some fundamentals, but I am a firm believer that it never hurts even if you are a skilled communicator to review the fundamentals.

Admittedly, the most fun reading is when you get to the Ninja Master Techniques because you will begin to feel like you're gaining a fun new superpower. Your awareness of things you missed in the past will suddenly become clear to you. For some people, they may even reflect on past conversations and relationships and have those "aha" moments.

While everyone has their own moral compass, I implore you not to use this information to hurt or negatively manipulate anyone, but to foster a clearer understanding and use your newfound skill sets as a force for uniting the people around you.

There will invariably be areas you are strong in, for example; one-on-one conversation, and other areas you want to work on; such as your public speaking techniques. This is where it's best to read through and get an understanding of the overall concept first and then read it again with a highlighter to capture key points and ideas. Re-read it as many times as it takes to make it an integrated part of your personality, this will make it effortless to command your environment with confidence.

Make it a point to use the techniques day to day, this allows you to form new habits in how you are communicating and interacting with others.

For those of you who are educators or work with young people it would bring great satisfaction if you were to make this book required reading for them. Our education system has remained the same for over 100 years, and while fundamental knowledge is important, not enough is being done to teach this new generation how to be effective communicators. These days modern communication has been reduced to meme's, emoji's and forty characters or less. In another generation, the art of communication will no longer exist in its present form, I believe we owe it to our children to teach them to be effective communicators.

> "Wise men speak because they have something to say; Fools because they have to say something."
>
> **Plato**

• MY STORY •

WHEN I DECIDED TO WRITE THIS BOOK, I went through a thought process like any other author; some have studied a subject their entire life, others have had profound experiences that shaped their perspective and made them uniquely qualified to write a book. I like to think I am a little bit of both and can say with certainty regardless of your education or training that by the time you finish this book you will learn some new things that will sharpen your communication skill sets and give you deeper insight into the art of communication. How can I be so certain? Because this is not a traditional book on communication, we are not going to cover one aspect of communication; we are going to examine several different sciences and what each one can teach us about how to convey ideas and what the person in front of us is telling us.

It is my hope that you will begin to see communication differently; as a holistic process that involves all of our senses and different perceptive powers that we all possess and simply need to develop. I would also encourage you to share this with your children and people you care about. I believe that if we can better understand each other, there will be less hate and intolerance in the world and that we will see each other's humanness and foster better relationships regardless of cultural, racial or religious differences. This is the hallmark of an evolved society. So, let me share a little of my story so that as you read you will appreciate certain insights I provide throughout this book.

    I was born in Costa Rica and my family is from a small town called Puerto Limon'. The primary language spoken in Costa Rica is Spanish, however in Limon' the small town we are from, a peculiar dialect is spoken called *Patois*. It is a form of broken English, a combination of French and English intermingled with certain Spanish words. To the American ear it would sound like a deep Jamaican accent, with some words that were simply unintelligible. When we arrived in the states, I was only four years old; everything was new and different. The people spoke what seemed to us a very strange dialect. By the time I started kindergarten it was evident to me that I was different because the children around me laughed when I spoke. My way of speaking embarrassed me so much that I became determined to master the King's English. I was fortunate at the time that a new show for kids came on called *Sesame Street*. I listened closely and began mastering the language quickly. As I grew older my passion for communication continued to grow and so, I devoured new vocabulary words and sentence structure, carried a dictionary around until it was yellow and dog-eared. I was now confident that at my early age I was an excellent communicator.

This early experience made me sensitive to how people reacted around me. I became a keen observer of human nature watching for behaviors that gave me insight to what someone might be thinking. By the time I was in high school my appetite for learning human nature had grown, I regularly read publications like *Psychology Today* the popular magazine at that time that gave me even greater insight to human behavior. I read books like *Your Erroneous Zones* written by Wayne Dyer back in 1976. I recall one occasion where I observed that when people disagreed they often rubbed their nose at the moment of disagreement. It wasn't until years later that I read in a new book that "new studies" had shown a correlation between nose scratching and disagreements. When I realized that many of my observations were being corroborated by psychologist, it confirmed my convictions that I was on the right track.

NINJA COMMUNICATIONS

Brush with History

There were other formative experiences that helped to shape my communication and reasoning skill sets. For instance, I grew up in the Bronx New York and in 1981 the American hostages were finally freed from Iran after 444 days in captivity. I belonged to Kips Bay Boy's Club and was asked to participate in a play about how the American hostages survived captivity in Iran. I was chosen as the lead in that play and was to give a rousing patriotic speech as part of my role. Unbeknownst to me and the other actors, news of the play was sent to the press, and two of the newly released American hostages decided to attend. Barry Rosen, one of the hostages and a native of Brooklyn, served as one of the main spokespersons for the hostages throughout the entire siege; he became a familiar face in NY. He had gotten word of the play and decided to come out and see it. I will never forget when I looked out at the audience that day, because Mr. Rosen chose to attend, there were news reporters, TV cameras and a massive crowd that had gathered. I remembered walking onto that stage completely terrified but determined to give honor to the brave men and women that were held captive for so long.

As the play progressed and I was to give my speech, I felt as if my heart was in my throat. My adrenaline was on overdrive and as I began to speak some power possessed me beyond my young experience at that time. I began to speak the words with power, clarity, confidence and passion. It felt as if some strange power had possessed me that I didn't know I had. By the time I had finished this emotionally charged monologue written by my mentor Dale Drakeford of Kips Bay Boys Club, the crowd stood to their feet began applauding and roaring in delight! The energy that I felt that day, imbued me with power and confidence that changed the trajectory of my life. After stepping off that stage and being congratulated and embraced by some of the tearful men that had experienced that difficult captivity, I came to believe that I *was* a public speaker. I was transformed from that young child from Costa Rica, unfamiliar with this language, to a confident public speaker that would never fear the stage again.

After that experience, my confidence as a public speaker grew rapidly; I went on to become the lead character in my high school play, I then joined a theater group in New York City and performed in off-Broadway plays and performances, I joined public speaking groups such as the ESS Club and Toastmasters. Through these experiences I was steadily honing my communication and public speaking skill sets.

When I went to college, I had another formative experience. I attended Iona College in New Rochelle NY, which was a Catholic-based college at the time. I was majoring in business and had to take a class in economics. I had a professor whose name now escapes me but left quite an impact. He was a mean and angry man even though he was a priest. He wore the traditional black and white collar of the catholic priests; he had piercing blue eyes, snow white hair, and a red ruddy, wrinkled complexion. He was a chain smoker and had the habit of humiliating his students by asking trick questions that they could not answer.

One day when I entered the classroom his piercing blue eyes locked on me, he decided that would be the day he would humiliate me. The subject was *Economics Supply and Demand*. He had a glass of water sitting on the table that had been partially filled with water. He looked at me with a menacing look and said, "Mr. Hines, is this glass of water half full or half empty?" I responded by saying, "I cannot answer that question." He turned slightly red and asked the question again, "Is the glass of water half full or half empty?" Once again with further resolve I said, "I can't answer that question." At this point he became visibly irritated, and he stated it again in a louder voice. "This is not a difficult question, we are not talking rocket science here, so answer the question; is this glass of water half full or half empty?" Once again with great conviction I said, "I *cannot* answer that question." His eyes narrowed on mine and he barked, "Why!?!" And I responded, "Because I don't know how the glass came to be at 50% capacity, if it were empty and you filled it to 50% before we came into the room, then it would be half full. On the other hand, if it were full, and you poured out 50% of its content then it would be half empty. So, until I know how the glass came to be at 50% capacity, I cannot answer the question!"

When I gave this clever answer, the class erupted in applause and I remembered watching that man literally bite down on the side of his hand in anger at the humiliation that was leveled at him by my response. This experience left an impression on me because despite tremendous pressure I decided to stay with my conviction even though this man had a PhD.

There is a fascinating footnote to the story; I later attended a public speaking and emotional development club that was fashionable among "Yuppies" in the early 1980s in New York City. Although I was quite young and not yet a Yuppie, I was asked to attend one of their meetings. While there each new person was asked to convey an experience that had impacted their life. I chose to tell that experience to a group, who were mostly in their 30's and 40's, upwardly mobile professionals. At the end of my story they all came up to me congratulating me on both my boldness and genius in the reasoning of that answer. But the story doesn't end there, fast-forward about 10 years later; I was watching the *Tonight Show with Johnny Carson.* That night Bill Cosby was the featured guest. I looked on in amazement as I watched Bill Cosby tell Johnny Carson *my story* and the audience burst into applause and Johnny laughed with delight. Of course, I tried to call the NBC Tonight Show studios to tell them that was actually my story, but I don't think they believed me because I never got a call back. That brush with history helped me to realize how the world appreciated clear reasoning and sound conviction.

Throughout the years I continued to hone my skills as a public speaker and then later in life, I joined a religious group and regularly did public talks in front of thousands of people. I was appointed as an elder who trained congregation members in how to give effective public talks. During the time, I taught these classes I gained deep insights on: the nuances of voice inflection, pausing for emphasis, power pace and pitch, developing effective metaphors and much more. It was the most effective training of my life. My journey as a communicator had come full circle, and here I was the "teacher". This amazing experience culminated in my giving a speech at the Houston Astrodome in front of 50,000 people.

These experiences helped me to develop my confidence and skill sets as an effective communicator and public speaker. I eventually started a business that led me to be on major radio stations throughout Houston and syndicated programs around the United States. As part of my business I decided to get trained and certified as an Energy Healer, Cranial Sacral Therapist, Matrix Energetics, and as a Holistic Naturopathic Practitioner. These trainings helped me understand how each of us are truly energy-based creatures. I learned how our bodies can heal naturally with the right nutrition, the proper thought processes, and effective healing modalities. This led me to gain greater insights in the mind-body connection and how what we communicate has power both physically and emotionally in our lives.

After going through a divorce and raising my three young children on my own, I have come full circle in my experiences over these many years. As of the time of this writing, I own Synergy Radio, commercial radio stations that cover all of Houston and surrounding areas. The stations focus on talk radio. Our mission is to create, "The Kind of Talk that Inspires Change." I also produce content for our digital TV studio called the *Genuine Journey Network,* which airs programs on *ROKU, Android TV and Amazon Fire*. We create original content, talk shows, mini documentaries, and other content that inspires people to live their best life. I am proud of my accomplishments throughout the years and realize that every one of these experiences is worth sharing with people like you. So now, it is a profound honor and a privilege to be able to present to you **Ninja Communications: The Art and Science of Influence**.

> "Words are singularly the most powerful force available to humanity. We can choose to use this force constructively with words of encouragement, or destructively using words of despair. Words have energy and power with the ability to help, to heal, to hinder, to hurt, to harm, to humiliate and to humble."
>
> **Yehunda Berg**

Communication, the Fabric of Our Existing

The ancient ninja was reputed to be amongst the most skilled warriors in the Eastern world. Their greatest strength was their ability to move with stealth, undetected. Their opponents and enemies never saw them coming. Skilled communicators understand that communicating your ideas and influencing the thoughts of others, requires stealth, and a highly developed awareness of those you are in front of. Modern communication is more than a one or two-dimensional exchange. In fact, as you read this book you will come to appreciate that all five of our senses are involved in our communication on a daily basis. When we learn to engage our sense of sight, sound, touch, and smell we get a very clear picture of the intention and thoughts of the person in front of us. The skilled communicator not only understands his audience, but through various clues can read their minds and in so doing, impact them in a much more profound and meaningful way.

• SECTION ONE •

Holistic Communication

IMAGINE FOR A MOMENT THAT YOU ARE about to walk into a pharmacy, just before you enter you see two teenagers run past you out of the store with a panicked look on their faces, clutching a woman's purse. As you walk in you see the store manager running after them yelling "hey stop!" The two boys hurriedly jumped into a car and skid out of the parking lot. Now hit the pause button for a moment. What do you think just happened? Most people would make the assumption that those teenagers just stole someone's purse and they are making their escape.

Ok, hit the play button again. You see the store manager and ask what happened. The store manager then explains that the two young men had to get insulin for their mother because she was having a hypoglycemic attack (low blood sugar). She sent her sons to get her prescription filled, but she didn't have time to find it so she told them to take her whole purse since she knows that the prescription is in there and just rush to the pharmacy. The store manager then explains that they forgot their receipt and prescription instructions, so he was trying to catch them before they left the store. The panicked look on the boy's faces was their fear for their mother's life.

If you witnessed this scene and didn't have the rest of the story, you would conclude the boys were up to no good. Once you understand the rest of the story, everything seemed to make sense and your perception has completely changed. In fact, you may now perceive these boys as hero's rather than villains.

This story is a good example of incomplete communication if you do not have all the information you can come to a wrong conclusion. If you only have half the story, it's easy to get it wrong. *Ninja Communications* is about, *holistic communication*, getting the entire story by understanding what's happening under the surface of a conversation. If you were watching a foreign language film without subtitles, you may be able to follow the story, but you would miss a lot of the nuances. A holistic approach to communication allows you to see those subtitles and adjust your approach in real time to get the desired outcomes.

Once you become a Ninja Communicator, you are regularly sharpening your observation, and listening skills, picking up on the non-verbal cues and applying some key techniques. When you learn how to read body language, voice inflection, facial expression, and other important context clues you will be a much more effective communicator. You may want to read this book with a highlighting pen and review certain parts several times to ensure that you really understand some of the key concepts. We will discuss some unique elements to assist you in mastering the *Art of Communication*.

The Importance of Effective Communication

With the exception of air, water, and food, communication is arguably the most important factor in our lives and the glue that holds civilizations together. To some this seems like an overstatement, but the fact is; communication is defined as the imparting or exchanging of information, ideas, and instruction. Understanding our past, making sense of our present, and building our future*, is, was*, and *will* always be based on some form of communication. When effective communication is used to convey ideas, those ideas can become infectious. They can grow, take root and change the world. Every world leader that has emerged in history had one thing in common, they were strong communicators. Successful companies are built on the basis of ideas and innovations that were communicated effectively and inspired teams that help that dream to grow.

We see the importance of communication everywhere in our personal lives. As soon as a child is born, instinctively parents begin communicating with that child. As the child grows, it is taught a language to communicate its feelings, its ideas, and most importantly the vital information for its survival.

In relationships between significant others, effective communication including love languages need to be understood clearly to ensure the growth and health of that relationship. In fact, the demise of the relationship usually begins when communication starts to break down. You will hear couples say things like, "we just grew apart" or "they are just not the same person". What has really happened here is that the communication has shifted and the couple feels like their connection has been lost.

When we first think of communication, the thought that comes to most people's mind is verbal communication. But in truth, communication takes many forms. As humans, we perceive and transmit messages using all five senses. Most people believe communication is taking place mostly with words, the fact is that communication is being transmitted through all of our senses at one time including our sense of smell, touch, and yes even taste. These varied forms of communication include: body language, touch, tone of voice, gestures, emotions, facial expressions and other nonverbal signals.

As we become aware of these different forms of communication, we start to understand the cues that are given to convey the feelings and thoughts of those we interact with daily. We will explore different aspects of communication and how you can master this important skill. It will help you to advance in your business life as a professional or entrepreneur, and in your personal life, with your spouse, your significant other, your children, your parents, your relatives, your friends, and those you interact with on a daily basis. It may even give you better insight in understanding yourself.

What Are the Various Forms of Communication?

Let's take a few moments to explore the various forms that communication takes. It's important to understand when thinking about communication that words are merely tools, but by no means the only part of communication. If you have a fully stocked toolbox, there would be tools such as screwdrivers, wrenches, pliers, hammers each serving a distinct purpose. It is possible to loosen or to tighten a nut with a pair of pliers, but anyone who has tried this quickly learns that pliers can destroy the edges of the nut and damage it for any further use. If, however, an exact ratchet or wrench is used then the nut can easily be loosened or tightened without damage, the same is true for words. The correct words can accomplish your objective; the wrong words can damage relationships. Mark Twain said it best, "The difference between the right word and the almost right word is the difference between lightning and a lightning bug."

NINJA COMMUNICATIONS

The words being used in communication can be likened to an iceberg that has its tip above the waters. To the casual observer that's all they see; yet below the surface, there is a huge body that remains to be discovered. The *body* of the iceberg hidden under those waters is the parts of communication that are conveyed in ways other than just the obvious words that are being used. These messages are cloaked in facial expressions, voice intonations, body language, and unique gestures that convey the bigger story. For many of us these nonverbal cues can go under the radar and unnoticed. Some may think, what does it matter if we miss a few of these little cues? One can argue that these cues albeit small could prevent major miscommunication and broken relationships, or perhaps even save a life.

Suppose your child was being bullied in school and felt overwhelmed, but you didn't notice this in their body language or facial expressions. What if your boss was under pressure and had to make the decision as to who he needed to lay off? Or maybe your girlfriend felt as though you were not being loving to her and she expressed this through her tone and body language; or your boyfriend was getting upset because something you said made him feel disrespected? Missing these cues could affect relationships or possibly lead to more serious circumstances. When we think about it that way, we can all benefit from improving our communications skill sets. Let us now explore a few different types of communication.

The first and most obvious form of communication is verbal communication. We put together words to convey ideas, to express feelings, to explore ideas, and to impart information to those we speak with. As we stated above communication is more than just the words that are used. *Effective* communication also depends on our tone of voice, our voice inflections, and the speed with which we speak. All of these are cues that give the listener a sense of our state of mind and our intention. Many people today communicate with text messaging. However, as many can attest, a text message can be easily misunderstood when we are not clear on the tone that the sender intended, perhaps this is the reason for the all too popular emoji's.

For example, if you received a text that says, "hey where have you been?" this could be taken very seriously, or the person could mean it in a funny, playful way, because they miss you. Without understanding the tone of the message, it can be easily misinterpreted. So, speech experts all agree that it is not always what you say but *how you say it*. Our voice inflections, the tone we use, as well as our *intentions*, go a long way in communicating our message.

How the listener perceives the message is also an integral part of communication. Listening is an active process. Watch others as they listen to good or bad news, you will notice it can affect the physical body in an instant.

For example, imagine you are at home relaxing and your telephone rings. There is a voice on the other end of the phone that says, "is this _____?" You respond, "yes, it is, who is this?" The voice continues, "this is Officer Jones, I'm calling regarding your mother. There's been a terrible accident...." Now, let's hit the pause button. In the moment you hear those words, your level of stress shoots up, your heart rate immediately increases, and your body feels weakened. You may even feel a cold sweat, or faint as you anticipate the next words to come out of the officer's mouth, but you immediately say, "what's happened?!?"

Now, less than thirty seconds has passed since you picked up the phone, yet what was once a relaxing evening is changed instantly by the words that were conveyed and the thoughts that fill your head when you listened to those words. The point of this illustration is that words can have a profound effect on the listener; listening *is* an *active process*.

Body language is another very powerful communicator. When we engage another person in conversation, we will either be consciously or subconsciously observing body language to see how our message is being received. For example, is the person nodding and in agreement with our statement, are their arms folded and are they wearing a frown, are they smiling and reacting with playfulness to our message? Each of these are very different responses conveying very different messages, yet none of them require verbal expression. They are all conveyed through the power of body language. It is important to use body language to communicate the right message when we speak as well as communicating the right message when we listen. We will delve into this deeper in a later chapter.

Another very powerful component in communication is emotion. Throughout history there are many examples of speakers that moved large numbers of people with passionate speech, such as Winston Churchill, Adolf Hitler, Martin Luther King Jr., and more recently Barack Obama and Donald Trump. Now regardless of whether you agree with their politics or not, each of these orators used emotion to affect the thinking of their audience. The strength of emotion is that it is contagious. When someone listens to passionate speech it is likely that they will have an emotional reaction to what is being said. We can think of emotion as the fire that heats the pot, it stirs the feeling of others and in many cases, moves them to take action.

NINJA COMMUNICATIONS

In our next chapter let's take a detailed look at the many different forms that communication can take.

> "Rough diamonds may sometimes be mistaken for worthless pebbles."
>
> **Thomas Browne**

• SECTION TWO •

The Many Facets of Communication

THE SKILLED COMMUNICATOR understands that communication has many facets. A useful metaphor might be to consider a diamond, what makes a diamond so beautiful are the facets that is cut into it. Each facet or face creates a beautiful prism of color that reflects light and brings beauty to the stone. If the diamond is uncut, it may resemble a worthless stone. So it is with effective communication. Communication is taking place on different levels all at the same time; the power is in seeing these levels and interpreting the light that is reflected. Some of these levels are:

a) Your Body Language,
b) Your Facial Expression,
c) Your Intonation and Voice Inflection,
d) Your emotional state,
e) Your energy,
f) Your pitch, power and pace,
g) Your willingness to listen,
h) Your pheromones,
i) Relational Vs. Transactional energy.

Each of these elements creates a tapestry, a composite that we call *communication*. Let's take a few moments to more closely examine each of these elements of communication.

Let's start our discussion by first addressing verbal communication. Before a child is born a mother instinctively begins speaking to her child. The child recognizes the voice of its mother and father before it exits the womb, and can hear everything happening in its immediate surroundings including music and other conversations. Auditory communication is not exclusive to humans; many animals use various forms of sound to signal warnings against approaching predators, mating calls, and sounds to direct their young. What makes human communication unique is the complexity and the large variety of words that not only communicate some of the basics but also conveys complex and abstract thought.

Basic Communication versus Intentional Communication

The key difference between most people that communicate versus professionals such as lawyers, politicians, spokespeople, or corporate heads, is that the professional communicator measures their words and understands the impact of the tools they choose to convey an idea. When a professional speaker begins to speak they must first understand their audience. For instance, if a speaker is a doctor, and he is speaking to other doctors he may use medical terms that are familiar to his audience. On the other hand, if he's speaking to a group of prospective patients, he may choose different terminology that is more comprehensible to the general public.

Another important factor in communicating certain words is making sure that we take into account regional dialects as well as colloquialisms that are unique to the group we are speaking with. Using the right, well-placed regional or cultural terms connects the speaker instantly to their audience and builds rapport, making them receptive to the group they're speaking to. On the other hand, using the wrong words or terms that alienate listeners can create mistrust and prevent the speaker from influencing the audience in the direction that they would like to take them.

We must recognize that words are tools that are used to create a desired outcome. When we speak intentionally we become very clear on what message we'd like the listeners to receive. Some people prefer extemporaneous speech or speaking off-the-cuff. An example of this was in the 2016 Presidential Elections, Donald Trump preferred speaking extemporaneously. He used this as a strength and claimed that his opponents had to use teleprompters because they were 'typical politicians that needed to follow a script'. In many respects, this served him because he brought something to the attention of his audience that many had not been thinking about. On the other hand, it got him in trouble at times because many things he said offended the listeners. When it comes to off-the-cuff speeches, it may be acceptable in some cases, but not advisable for the non-skilled speaker. If you've ever observed someone in front of an audience who is nervous and attempts to speak extemporaneously, you will notice they have a tendency to reveal things that they did not intend to reveal. If you speak when unprepared, this can completely undermine your efforts to effectively communicate the message to your audience.

The best way to avoid this is to commit certain keywords and phrases to memory then build your talk around those key phrases to ensure the proper messages. Using bullet points or an outline is the best way to achieve this goal.

Body Language and Nonverbal Communication

One of the most important aspects of communication is nonverbal. Let's take a few moments to explore the important world of body language. Scientists all agree that the subconscious mind is processing a substantial amount of information beneath the surface of conscious thinking. According to some studies, the subconscious mind processes about 400 billion bits of information per second compared to the conscious mind that processes about 2000 bits per second.* This means that the moment we enter another person's presence or begin to listen and observe them we are taking in billions of bits of information, far more than the words that are coming out of their mouth. The commonly held belief is that:

- 55% of communication is body language
- 38% is the tone of voice
- 7% is the actual words spoken

An important addendum to this statistic is that certain other factors must be taken into account such as the context, the clusters, and congruence. That is to say, what is the environment and situation as well as the history between the people and the roles that each of those individuals play, such as superior or subordinate?

A person's body language is generally a byproduct of subconscious thinking, which means, they don't actually think about *how* they are holding or moving their bodies in certain situations. Therefore, our subconscious body language can be a very accurate barometer to what we really are thinking. The way we move our bodies, our facial expressions, our voice intonations and other subtle indicators can create a very accurate picture as to what our true intentions or beliefs are.

Some researchers believe that this innate ability to read another person's physical motion is a remnant from the limbic brain (primitive brain) when we relied less on speech and more on movement to decode the intentions of a potential friend or adversary. Regardless of its origins, the fact is that it does exist, and your ability to interpret these signals gives you a decided advantage when communicating with others.

How someone moves their body is very distinct to the individual, and in many cases their gender. For example, even from a distance if you observed a person's walk you could make a pretty accurate guess as to whether they were male or female. Whether someone is speaking or listening their body language speaks volumes about how they are receiving your message or what they are truly attempting to communicate.

For example, social dominance is often displayed through body language. Psychologists have discovered that the length of time eye contact is maintained is a direct correlation to a person's social status. In other words, if you're the boss you tend to stare directly in the eyes of your subordinates twice as long as if you are a subordinate looking into the eyes of your boss. This is known as 'eye dominance' which will be explored further in our discussion.* Another common nonverbal cue is given when a person is ready to conclude a conversation they will shift their body language towards the nearest exit and will give additional signals to indicate they are ready to conclude the conversation.

More obvious signs are seen when a speaker is making a good point and their audience begins to nod vigorously, or perhaps they are in disagreement and they fold their arms and tilt their heads away from the speaker. It is important to remember, however that nonverbal communication is not a language with a fixed set of meanings. There are variables that influence how things can be interpreted which include the place and the people concerned as well as the culture. Cultural influences can play a large role in how gestures and body language is interpreted.

In Italy and in many Spanish or Latin countries, gestures are a very integral part of communication. But in certain parts of Europe like the United Kingdom gestures are not used as frequently, and for some it's interpreted as a lack of sophistication or control. In the United States giving the thumbs-up is an indication that everything is great, but if you happen to be in Greece, Italy or Iran and give the thumbs-up it may be interpreted as an insult; like Americans interpret the middle finger. This is helpful information if you will be traveling or speaking abroad, it may prevent some embarrassment if you take a few moments to explore the culture and some of the local gestures.

As part of this topic there is another way we can get to know our significant other, our coworkers, our subordinates or our superiors. This deals with *how they listen*. For example, when a third party is speaking; carefully observe *how* others are listening to what is being said. In many cases, since the listeners do not believe that *they* are being observed they are less guarded, and as such their body language tends to reveal a considerable amount about their thinking. This is also experienced when two people just start dating and they sit and watch a movie, *how* they respond to what they are seeing on screen, as well as facial expressions can reveal a lot about that person's way of thinking in regular day-to-day situations.

There is much to be said on the subject of body language in both business and social situations. For instance, many people hate going to networking events when they don't know anyone. As a Ninja Communicator, I enjoy it. There are always people in the room that are awkwardly standing around wishing someone would approach them and strike up a conversation. I notice those people immediately. Of course, sometimes the challenge you have is ending the conversation since they are not comfortable approaching someone else when you are done talking to them.

In social situations, effective body language reading could open up your entire world to new relationships. I personally love to Salsa Dance, I recall going out one evening and I observed a beautiful woman, who was watching others having fun on the dance floor. For those who don't know how to salsa dance, it is intimidating because it is a series of complex spins and turns and foot work that requires a bit of coordination. As I observed this beautiful girl, her body language suggested that she would love to join in but lacked the confidence as a novice to just put herself out there. I approached her and said, "Let me guess, you're an expert dancer and no one in here can match your brilliance on the dance floor?" Of course, I was being totally sarcastic, and she laughed and said, "No, just the opposite. I'd love to learn but this is kind of intimidating." I smiled confidently extending my hand and said, "Follow my fingers and in a few minutes, I will have you dancing like an expert." We got on the dance floor, I kept my promise and she had the time of her life. We ended up dating for several years after that and had a wonderful relationship. The moral of the story, *Reading Body Language effectively can change your life!*

When we consider body language and nonverbal communication, it is important to remember that nonverbal communication is more of a composite or series of different motions and gestures that are tied together to create a total picture. For us to become effective in our interpretation of body language we must look at the context, the circumstances, and the relationship that we have with the speaker or those whom we are attempting to communicate with.

There is much more to the topic of body language that we can explore, in our chapter on *Ninja Master Communication Techniques* we will further explore some fun and unique ways we can practically read the minds of those we communicate with.

> "False eloquence is exaggeration; true eloquence is emphasis."
>
> ## William R. Alger

Intonation and Emphatic Speech

Earlier in this chapter we mentioned that potentially 38% of communication could be tone of voice, to some this may seem like a bit of an overstatement. The old expression 'it's not what you say but how you say it', is quite true. We cannot understate the importance of voice tone in communicating messages. In fact, at its very core voice intonation can communicate more directly than actual words. Tone of voice can reveal different aspects of our emotion for instance: sarcasm, superiority, submissiveness, anger, or humor.

Let's consider a few examples. When we are speaking to an infant from the very point of birth, instinctively most people will speak in a soft, soothing voice to elicit a friendly or happy response. At the early stages of life, the infant does not yet know what words truly mean so his reactions are based solely on tone of voice. If the voice is warm and friendly, the child may begin to smile; if the voice is harsh or abrupt, the child may begin to cry.

Our pets are also a good example of the importance of voice tone in communication. Try this simple experiment if you have a dog. Say to them in a very kind, loving, cheerful tone; *you're a bad dog, and I'm going to make you sleep outside tonight because you're such a bad dog.* Now if this was said in a warm, cheerful, loving way your pet would likely wag his tail and come to you to be petted. Now let a few moments go by and say to your pet in a harsh, abrupt and aggressive tone; *you're a good dog, and I'm going to get you some doggie treats because I love you so much.* If you said these words in a hostile, aggressive manner your pet would put back his ears, put his tail between his legs and try to get away from you. This is a pretty clear indicator that the dog is responding more to your tone than to your words.

Tone of voice also plays a significant role in our relationships with our significant other. When we want to convey affection to our love interest, we speak in a soft, reassuring tone. If we are disappointed in something they have done or said, our tone will denote that even before words have completely been spoken. We see examples of this all the time. We may utter one or two words and immediately our significant other says, "What's the matter with you?"

Our tone of voice and the way we modulate can affect the behavior of those around us. For example, when disciplining children some mothers have wondered how they could speak repeatedly to their children and they simply will not listen, yet when the father says the same thing one time, the children are quick to listen and do what they're told. Of course, they may see the father as a strong authority figure, but some believe that a lower tone of voice is also associated with greater authority.

When George HW Bush ran for president in 1988, he hired a voice coach to help drop his tone by an octave. Now why was this so important? Although he fought in World War II, hailed as a war hero and he was head of the CIA, due to the higher pitch in his voice, his adversaries and critics perceived him as a *"wimp"*. This crystalizes the importance of voice intonation when wanting to be authoritative, begin to practice a lower tone and speak a bit slower and more emphatically. Making this slight adjustment in voice tone and speed of speech, your message takes on greater authority and weight.

The reason that voice intonations are so crucial in communication is due to the fact that more than any other part of speech, intonation communicates your emotional state. Emotion is contagious when listening to a speaker. An attentive audience will subconsciously reflect the emotional disposition of the person they are listening to. The skilled speaker understands to truly impact their audience they must embody the emotions in the words they speak.

When it comes to sales, it has been proven consistently that successful salespeople have a positive upbeat tone of voice, their tone tends to convey positive emotions to their listener. In fact, it is a common practice at telemarketing call centers to have little signs on their desks that says, "remember to keep a smile in your voice". This little reminder sends an immediate signal to the person on the other end of the phone that they are speaking with someone that is likable and worth listening to. The successful salesperson or one who is skilled with social intelligence will also incorporate a bit of humor and levity with an upbeat positive tone of voice. This combination is a very effective rapport builder, and can make the difference between someone listening or quickly dismissing you as an unwelcome interruption.

Word Emphasis

Another important element in proper communication is placing emphasis on the proper words. Emphasis creates depth and meaning in communication. Skilled speakers understand the importance of proper word emphasis.

Many public speakers will use a highlight pen to highlight those words they need to "punch" or emphasize to communicate their points. When words are given the proper emphasis, and fueled with the right level of emotion, they become powerful tools in conveying ideas and swaying a listener to accept your point of view. Just by changing what word is emphasized you can alter the meaning of your message significantly. For example, read the following statement and change where you place the emphasis on the italicized word:

He said he had to think about your proposal.
He *said* he had to think about your proposal.
He said he had to *think* about your proposal.

He said he had to think about **your** proposal.

He said he had to think about your ***proposal.***

In each case when the word emphasized changed, the meaning to the listener's ear also changed; either slightly or significantly. Understanding the power of emphasis, we must underscore the proper words to accurately convey the meaning of our statements.

Voice and Modulation

Another aspect of emphasis is voice modulation. We can change our speed or volume to create different points of emphasis, this is an excellent technique to keep listeners engaged. There's an old expression that says, "the difference between a good speech and a bad speech, is a comfortable nap." To avoid boring our audience, we should modulate our tone, pace and pitch; this keeps our listeners focused on our message.

When it comes to public speaking, we can liken an excellent speech to an amazing piece of music. A well-composed piece of music has a strong hook that stays in the listener's mind right from the beginning. It also moves the listener emotionally and builds to a crescendo. When the speaker reaches the crescendo in their talk, they should have the audience absolutely wrapped in every word they say. There are different techniques to hit a powerful crescendo. Let's consider some of those techniques:

- Start out speaking softly and slowly and build your volume and intensity.
- Introduce a key phrase then repeat it over and over while building greater depth and definition around the phrase.
- Use a powerful story to bring your key point to life.
- Speak with energy and enthusiasm, then drop to a whisper when you're making your key point.
- If you are trying to invoke emotion, create that emotion in your voice intonation.

There are many other techniques, the ones you choose to use depends on the content and subject matter of your presentation. Whichever you choose, be certain to infuse it with emotion, change up your pace, power and pitch. This will keep your audience engaged, and when you reach your crescendo use gestures and voice inflections to create a powerful impression.

> "The right word may be effective, but no word was ever effective as a rightly timed pause."
>
> ## Mark Twain

The Power of the Pause

Another technique that is very powerful and important to mention is using the power of pausing. A well-placed pause can serve multiple purposes. For the novice speaker, pausing will help them compose their thoughts, and help to minimize word whiskers such as: "Umm, huh, aah and OK". If you have the tendency to use these word whiskers in speech, try using a brief pause instead of filling the air with these meaningless word fillers. It is recommended that you record your speeches to become aware of when these word fillers are being used. Another important use for the pause is to create emphasis. It gives the audience a few seconds to absorb what they have just been told. To maximize the impact of this pause, the speaker should make their point, stop talking, and then stare out at the audience for a few seconds. This makes it clear to the audience that an important point was just made. If you must use notes try not to pause when looking down at your notes, this sends a message to your audience that you are not thoroughly prepared. Instead, memorize some transitional statements and glance at your notes while you are still speaking so that it creates a seamless transition. In a later chapter, we will also discuss the power of silence in getting others to reveal themselves.

> "When dealing with people, remember you are not dealing with creatures of logic, but creatures of emotion."

Dale Carnegie

The Power of Emotional Speech

If words are the vehicle, think of emotion as the fuel. Without fuel the vehicle cannot move forward, and as it pertains to speech, we cannot move our audience to consider our ideas if they are delivered without emotion. It is said that **80%** of the choices Americans make are emotionally driven, only 20% are governed by logic.*

There's an old acronym; H.A.L.T. which states that you should never make a decision while feeling **H**ungry, **A**ngry, **L**onely, or **T**ired. If you do, you will make an *emotional* decision **100%** of the time. Additionally, we cannot underestimate the influence the subconscious mind has on how someone listens. For example, there was an experiment done where some people were given cold beverages to hold in their hands while others were given warm beverages, then they were asked to describe a fictitious character. Those holding the colder beverages consistently viewed the character as cold and unfriendly. Understanding how the subconscious can influence an audience's thinking is important whether you're one-on-one trying to close a business deal or in front of thousands trying to make a very important point.

Some psychologists believe that when it comes to making decisions our right and left brain are constantly at war. When you walk into a car dealership, the practical side of your brain (left) is telling you to buy the economic, reliable car, but the creative, artistic, impulsive side (right brain) is telling you that you *absolutely need* that hot red sports car. Now which side will win? As the old adage goes, it depends on which side you feed. Advertisers understand this all too well. Commercials are designed to appeal to our emotions, stimulate our senses, and induce us to take action.

Now Madison Avenue has spent hundreds of millions of dollars to figure this out and the strategy has not changed for over 100 years. So, when it comes to moving people to action we don't try to reinvent the wheel, we simply hone our craft as speakers to move people to action by inducing their emotion. When it comes to getting our audience to do what we would like them to do, there is no more powerful tool than connecting with their emotions. Tune in to radio and TV commercials, you will notice that consistently they will appeal to your emotions, before they appeal to the logic. Always remember the words are the vehicle, but emotions are the fuel.

Sales and the Power of Emotion

When it comes to sales, the top producer understands this very important strategy. The first thing that a top closer does is builds rapport and establishes common ground. The second step is to ask questions and understand a person's needs. This period of *discovery* is where the skilled salesperson gets to understand the emotional hot buttons he will need to press to get his prospect to buy. When speaking one-on-one, each time an emotional button is pressed a trial close or what's also known as a "tie down" can be used. A few examples of tie downs are:

- Makes sense, doesn't it?
- You would agree with that, wouldn't you?
- That's a good way to think of it, right?
- Do you see how that would benefit you?
- Would you agree with me that _____?

These tie downs ensure that the listener agrees with your proposition and makes it difficult for them to say no when you get to the final close. If you are a sales person, you should memorize these and other tie downs and make them part of your regular presentation. Even if you are not a salesperson, every day you are making sales; you may be convincing your boss to accept a proposal, you may be trying to get a promotion, you might be writing an instructional manual, helping a patient or client to understand a new product your company offers or any other number of scenarios where these important techniques will apply.

> "Listening, not imitation, may be the sincerest form of flattery."
>
> ## Joyce Brothers

• SECTION THREE •

Listening, an Active Process

THERE'S AN AMUSING QUOTE THAT SAYS, "*Modern Communication in the 20th century, can best be described; as 'The one who takes a breath first, is declared the listener!'*".

Although this quote was written nearly a half a century ago, it is truer today than when it was coined. Some humorists that observe the communication culture in the 21st century referred to it as the age of ADD & ADHD (*Attention Deficit Disorder*). The average person looks at their phone 150 times per day according to a survey done back in 2013 and has increased steadily. News programs have been reduced to fast moving graphics and soundbites, most people today read blogs instead of books.

According to a study done by researcher Adler Rosenfeld it was determined that adults spend an average of

70% of their time engaged in some form of communication, of this an average of 45% was spent listening compared to 30% spent speaking, 16% reading and 9% writing.* This is a clear indication that reading is on the decline.

It is easy for us to begin speaking from our own point of view, but to be an effective speaker we must follow the words of the great sage who said... *'Seek first to understand before trying to be understood'*.

Highly developed listening skills will automatically raise your social intelligence IQ. *Effective listening* is one of the *most important* aspects of an effective communicator. Some may confuse *hearing* with *listening,* but these are quite different. It is one thing to hear sounds, it is another to *listen* and *comprehend*. Listening is not only paying attention to the story or what is being said, but also; *how* it is told, *what* type of language is being used, the *way* that the language is being expressed by the speaker, the *type* of voice intonations that color and shade the meanings, as well as focusing on other nonverbal cues to discern the speaker's *intent*. Your true competence as a listener is determined by your ability to perceive and understand not only *what* the speaker is saying but what *ideas* they are trying to convey. Often times when someone else is speaking we may have a tendency to work on formulating our response rather than actually listening closely to the idea the speaker is trying to convey. Whether this is our habit in our personal or professional life, it can affect critical relationships in a very adverse way. Let's take a few moments to consider 10 key principles to listening effectively.

Ten Key Principles to Effective Listening

- Focus on what's being said and put other thoughts out of your mind.
- Nod and use other nonverbal cues to encourage the speaker to feel comfortable.
- Let go of your filters and try to listen from the speaker's point of view.
- Take into account any accents or regional dialects when listening.
- Don't be quick to interrupt, give your speaker time to formulate their thoughts.
- Watch body language carefully to determine the speaker's intent.
- Look at their eyes to discern the conviction of their words.
- Look for inconsistencies in their words if contradicted by their nonverbal communication.
- Take in the entire message so that you can grasp the *idea* the speaker is conveying.
- Ask questions if you need clarification.

You should carefully consider each of the principles listed above and ask yourself if you truly apply these practices in your listening skill set. If you do not, then it's important to work on these practices until you have them mastered. These listening skill sets will make you a more effective communicator because you can better craft your message once you understand the audience you are speaking with. It will also make you more cognizant of how you are being perceived by your audience when you speak.

Reticular Activating System - Understanding How the Brain Processes Information

Another aspect of listening we need to consider; is not just how we listen but *how* others are listening to us. To gain a better understanding of how others hear us, it is important to get some insight on how the brain receives information.

At any given time during your daily activities you are being bombarded with millions of bits of sensory stimulation, everything from the sounds outside your window to the radio playing in the other room, to the messages popping up on the side of your computer screen while you're typing an email. Sounds, smell, taste, sight, feelings are all continually being downloaded from the environment around you. If we constantly had to process every single bit of information coming in from all five of our senses, we would easily be overwhelmed. The brain has an ingenious system that acts as a filter to control the things we focus on; that filter is called the **Reticular Activating System** (R.A.S.).

This brilliant part of the brain is about the size of your pinky, yet it serves a very crucial function. We have all experienced how it works. Let's say you buy a new car and it's a red Jaguar, and prior to buying it you didn't see too many of these on the road, yet after your purchase you notice them everywhere. Now does that mean that the moment you purchase the car everyone else decided to buy one, too?

Of course not, what has happened is that you activated your *Reticular Activation System,* and now your brain is focused on something that's important to it. This system works like a heat seeking missile to tune in to anything that is important to you. If you're in the market for a new house, all of a sudden, you're going to start noticing real estate signs everywhere.

It can also have the opposite effect by working like a powerful filter. For example, if you had a tennis net, and you took a handful of marbles and drop them onto the net, they would easily fall through. Conversely, if you take a basketball and dropped it onto the net, it would not penetrate. In this case, the marbles can be likened to the thoughts that are not important to you; your brain will virtually ignore these thoughts. The basketball on the other hand, would represent the things that are important to you; it will immediately connect with your conscious mind. This is all happening subconsciously without you being aware of it. This unique system keeps us focused on what is important to us while eliminating all the static in the air around us.

Another way the R.A.S. system can be activated is when we *consciously* filter something out of our mind. Let's say you're driving to work and you have cloth seats in your car, and you accidentally spill coffee on the passenger seat. You immediately think: *when I get home tonight I need to use some fabric cleaner to get rid of that stain.* That night you end up working late so you can't get to the stain. The next morning you notice it again and think: *I've got to get that cleaned up*. Things come up and after a week you just tune it out because it was annoying you.

Now you can no longer see the stain, but a coworker is getting in your car and immediately they look at your seat and say, "Hey, did you know you have a stain on your seat?" They can immediately see what you no longer can. When a person has a blind spot, the ophthalmologist will diagnose it as a condition called a **Scotoma**, this is defined *as a partial* *loss of vision or blind spot in an otherwise normal visual field.* We can develop a scotoma and no longer see what's right in front of us when the R.A.S. has been activated.

Understanding other people have a *Reticular Activating System* that can create a *scotoma,* is very important insight to being an effective speaker. Using the above analogy, your audience may not be able to see "the stain on *their* seat". If your audience does not understand they *have* a problem, challenge, or issue, then they can tune you out because they don't believe what you're saying applies to them. So, it is important to ask the right questions before you address an audience to understand *where* their scotoma could be. Then you set the framework by first defining their challenges and making them aware that they may have some issues. You can only accomplish this goal if you *listened carefully* to discern what their possible issues might be.

As part of this understanding you must recognize that a person's perception *can be* their reality. In other words, if they view the world as being a threatening dangerous place, and that no one can be trusted, then you and your words could be viewed as a threat.
If you do not build trust *before* you begin communicating your message, their filters will prevent your message from getting through to their heart. This is a universal truth of

communication and it applies in virtually every situation. Whether you are addressing a group in a business setting, speaking one-on-one to your children or someone you love, it is helpful to understand how they will perceive the message so that you can craft it in a way that is palatable to *their* ear.

Listening is indeed a very critical part of communication. There are a few other right brain, left brain techniques that we will discuss in an upcoming chapter on how to listen effectively.

"There are three methods to gaining wisdom. The first is reflection, which is the highest. The second is imitation, which is the easiest. The third is experience, which is the bitterest."

Confucius

• SECTION FOUR •

Becoming a Ninja Master in The Art of Communication

Advanced Ninja Communications Techniques

I LIKE TO REFER TO THEM AS *The Ninja Master Techniques*. As mentioned at the beginning of this book, when we think of a Ninja we think of a skilled warrior that has been trained in the art of stealth. Your ability to secretly observe the people you are speaking with and understand their unspoken words will give you a definitive advantage in your communication with them. Some of this material is based on the science of right and left-brain processing. Some based on the experience of professional public speakers and communicators. To give you a personal advantage in your interpersonal skill sets,

I recommend that you keep most of this information confidential so that you can exercise an advantage over those you are speaking to. Let's begin Ninja Communications.

> *"We either live with intention or exist by default."*
>
> ## Kristin Armstrong

Intentional Communication

An essential part of ninja communication is to learn how to speak *intentionally.* What exactly does that mean? The word intentional means something done on purpose or deliberately.

We need to be clear on what we *intend* as an outcome. Are we interested in a client accepting our proposal? Do we want our subordinates to show support for a new project? Would we like a person we have an attraction toward to develop mutual attraction? There's an old Russian proverb that says, "In times of peace, prepare for war." Before a conversation with someone it is a good practice to sit and even write out what you would like your desired outcome to be.

Why is this important? When we become clear on our *intentions,* we send a message to our subconscious mind to transmit those intentions in a number of subliminal ways to the person or group we focus on. This clear intention changes *how* we express our ideas, our body language, our passions and the very force and nature of our character which influences our audience. Clear intention is powerful. It activates your power of influence to such a degree that your audience, whether an individual or group, will sense your conviction and be moved to do what you intend for them.

When you first connect with your audience, whether it's an individual or a group, greet them in a way that prepares them for your conversation with them. People will always be more receptive to you if they think you care about them personally. If your demeanor is cold impersonal and detached, if you appear to be uncomfortable, angry or confrontational, these "tells" will put your audience on the defensive. If on the other hand they are greeted warmly, courteously, or at the very least professionally, you automatically have increased their level of receptivity to what comes out of your mouth next.

Intentional communication can have powerful results once you become clear on what you want. In some cases that clarity can save you time, money or emotional distress. I recall a few years ago; I dropped off a friend at night in an area I was unfamiliar with. It was dark, and as I was turning back on the main road to the highway, my phone distracted me for a few seconds. When I turned onto the main road, I went wide and slightly entered the oncoming lane of traffic. I quickly adjusted my course, but unfortunately, the car headed towards me was a police officer. He turned on his lights and rapidly made a U-turn to pull me over. As soon as I stopped, I immediately began focusing my thoughts on my intention; not getting a ticket. When he approached my vehicle, I looked him directly in the eyes and said, "Officer, let me explain what just happened." I then told him that I was getting treated for a neck spasm, thought the problem was under control, but got a painful spasm as I was turning onto the main road. The entire time I told my story; I looked him straight in the eye and focused my intention on him letting me off without writing me a ticket.

He ran my driver's license and insurance, came back to the vehicle and it appeared that he was going to write me up. Then, inexplicably he said, "I suggest you get off the road until your neck injury has been treated properly." Even as he was saying these words, it appeared as though he was speaking against his will. I believe he was fully prepared to write a ticket, but something shifted in his conscious mind and he let me off the hook. I believe that his subconscious was influenced by my clear intention not to receive a ticket. Perhaps you've had similar experiences where a person you were dealing with had one set of intentions, and then they suddenly shifted. The next time this happens, pay closer attention, it might just be your intention at work.

> "One can state, without exaggeration, that the observation of and the search for similarities and differences are the basis of all human knowledge."
>
> ## Alfred Nobel

Watch the Listener for Early Signs of Approval or Disapproval

It is important to practice honing your skill of observation even as you speak. The person or group you are speaking with will send nonverbal cues early in the conversation to indicate whether they are receiving your message in a positive or negative manner. If you see indications in body language or facial expressions such as; face tightening, brow wrinkling, jaws set in a clenched manner, arms folded, nose rubbing, these are indicators that your message is not being received well. At this point, you may want to ask a question or change your approach so that you can shift their state and interrupt their pattern. Unless you interrupt their pattern, they will continue to resist the message you are conveying. Once they are entrenched in resistance, they are no longer hearing anything else you say because their opinion has been formed and it will not be favorable to you.

If you have bad news, or some form of criticism that you need to convey to your listener, then it's best to use the sandwich approach. The way the sandwich approach works is you start with a compliment or some positive statement, then you deliver your criticism or bad news, then you close with another positive comment or means to give the listener hope.

For example, you might say, "Susan, I really appreciate and see all the hard work you've been doing to make this project work." Give her a moment to acknowledge your appreciation, then say, "when I checked some of the numbers they are not aligning properly with the early projections we made, so we need to revisit this to make sure we are accurate for the client." At this point, watch Susan's body language very closely. Is she open to this criticism or is her posture shifting to a defensive position? If she appears defensive then you may want to ask her, "are there other factors that we need to consider?" At this point, she will likely agree to reassess the project and make the adjustments, or she may be summing up the courage to defend her position. Her body language will tell you exactly which directions her thoughts are going, and you can adjust your approach accordingly. If she appears to agree with your assessment, you then conclude the conversation by saying, "I have a great deal of confidence in you and know you can make this work, please let me know what support you need from me, to help us to close this contract."

If done correctly, Susan will respect the way the conversation was handled and will work twice as hard to make things work because you've expressed confidence in her competence. The sandwich approach has been used for years and continues to be an effective way to reduce resistance to your message before it is delivered. Another important point to glean from the above example is that your language should reflect "we, us, our", and other such inclusive language. When we use inclusive language, it gives your listener the sense that you're in this with them and they have your support. If on the other hand you are saying, "I, me, you", and other individualistic language this can also put your listener on the defensive. Be sure to practice observing nonverbal cues to see how your listener is receiving your message. If they are in agreement or they seem neutral, then begin using "tiedowns."

Use "Tiedowns" when You Present Your Case

As mentioned previously in the Sales and Power of Emotion section, tiedowns are very effective ways to gain agreement and consensus as you move through your presentation. You can use this one-on-one or with an audience. Each time you make a key point, slowly nod your head up and down while using a tiedown.

- That makes sense doesn't it?
- You would agree with that wouldn't you?
- Do you see how that would benefit you?
- Are you seeing how that approach will help you gain ground?
- We can all agree on that right?

These and questions like these, carefully placed at the end of your key points, can be very effective. You will want to add the appropriate nonverbal cues; which would include open palms and a head that nods 'yes'. As you're making your points, your prospects or audience will begin to subconsciously agree with you and you can move them towards your point of view.

Top salespeople understand the power of this technique. The ability to include the nonverbal cues will magnify the effect significantly. There is actually a science behind this methodology, which deals with a part of the brain called the mirror neuron.

The Secret of the Mirror Neuron

A key factor to being a *Ninja Communicator* is understanding the secrets of the *Mirror Neuron.* Let us take a few moments to explain what it is. Fairly recent research has discovered a special class of brain cells that fire up when they observe another person performing an action. Notice how a baby reacts when someone smiles; it tends to smile back. Or have you ever been in a room where one person yawns and suddenly several other people begin yawning. Now does that mean that a smile or a yawn is contagious? Well, yes, in a manner of speaking. The mirror neuron causes humans and some animals to mimic behaviors that they are observing. This same system also allows us to decode facial expressions whether we are observing a specific expression or making it ourselves.

This research has determined the better we are at interpreting facial expressions the more active our mirror neuron system.

These findings show that the mirror neuron plays a key role in our ability to empathize and socialize with others because we are communicating our emotions *through* our facial expressions. The research further showed that people with autism or other conditions such as Asperger's syndrome tend to have a dysfunctional mirror neuron system and are limited or unable to decode social cues that help in day-to-day interaction.*

Have you ever met a person that just doesn't seem to have any "social intelligence"? They are completely oblivious to the non-verbal cues that others communicate? If you've seen this and thought to yourself, that person doesn't have a clue; it might be because they have a defective mirror neuron system. This research gives us great insight in the field of communication. Because in effect, we are all neurologically connected since our behaviors are mirrored by these special cells. A metaphor we can apply to understand this using modern technology is that we are all *wirelessly connected (Wi-Fi)*. If you work in an office, you may find that if the boss walks in and he's in a bad mood that mood quickly spreads throughout the office, or the opposite could also be true.

Have you ever noticed the general attitude in the office on a Friday versus a Monday? This gives greater importance to maintaining a positive disposition at all times which will be mirrored by those around you due to this neurological Wi-Fi. So, let's now discuss how we use the mirror neuron to influence others.

When speaking one-on-one you may want to try the mirroring technique. Here's how it works. You assume the general posture and body language of the person you are speaking with, particularly while you're listening. Then as you begin speaking, change your body language and watch if they mirror your behavior. For example, do they cross their legs towards you, do they begin to lean into you, are they showing smiles or nodding empathetically? These "tells" give you a clear indication as to whether or not you are influencing that person.

In public speaking, you can accomplish something similar by transmitting your emotions. Enthusiasm is contagious. As you get on stage, create an enthusiastic energy and engage your audience by asking questions. The questions may be rhetorical such as, "how's everyone feeling this morning?" Or "true or false, knowledge is power?" When stated with enthusiasm you can engage your audience and they will begin to mirror your enthusiasm and be more of an avid listener to your presentation.

An interesting part of the research as it gains popularity; is that the mirror neuron generally does not fire in the brain whenever it observes a trivial act; such as a mime or meaningless gesture or pantomimes. The synaptic firings in the brain connected to the mirror neurons will *only be activated when there is action that is significant and meaningful to it*. This gives credence to our earlier discussion of being *intentional* in your communication. When we begin to operate with the understanding that all of us, whether aware or not, are communicating partially using the mirror neuron, then we can more accurately craft our speech and actions to reflect the desired outcome we want in others. Although these theories are relatively new, just a little over a decade old as of the time of this publication, researchers are not all in agreement of the full function of the neural mirror neuron, but none are denying that it exists, and that it affects behavior.

A major part of the brain's emotional makeup is commonly referred to as the limbic brain. It consists of a number of different parts, many of which make up the emotions and memories that we have deep within us. When a speaker can effectively touch the emotions of his listeners, the effect is magnified significantly. Now that you are aware of the secret of the mirror neuron, be mindful when crafting your presentation to always keep your finger on the pulse of the limbic brain it will serve you well in getting the results you seek.

"Follow your intuition, listening to your dreams, your inner voice to guide you."

Katori Hall

Intuition, the Sixth Sense

All of us at one time or another have experienced a moment when our intuition saved us from potentially costly or even dangerous situations. My own personal experience with intuition has saved me more times than I can count.

One instance that stands out in my mind, took place back in the early 90s when I had the opportunity to purchase a Modeling and Acting School called APM Studios. At the time, the school's claim to fame was that they were the school that trained the famous Calvin Klein Jean Model turned Reality Star, the late Anna Nicole Smith.

I had signed on as Director of the school, and under my leadership it was now generating as much as $20,000 a week! The owner of the school congratulated me on my successes and asked if I would be interested in buying the school. I was confused as to why he would sell a profitable entity. He explained, his first love was photography and now he was close to retirement and didn't want the pressures of continuing to run the school. When I looked at the numbers and what he was willing to sell the school for, it appeared to be the deal of a lifetime. My initial reaction was sheer excitement, but there was an annoying feeling in my lower gut that simply would not go away. Despite the research and vetting process, I had been doing when considering the purchase, all of which made this deal look very favorable, in my core I kept feeling as if something was wrong.

I finally came to the painful decision to not go forward with the purchase of the school. At the time, it would have been a culmination of one of my dreams to help young people improve self-esteem and self-identity; not to mention the possibility of making me very rich. Instead, I started a business in a completely different industry.

Fast-forward, a year later I received a phone call from a gentleman identifying himself as the person that purchased the modeling and acting school. Let's call him Jim. He asked if

I would meet with him. Jim was a medium built, red-headed man who was professionally trained as a CPA, who quickly ushered me into his office. His body language and demeanor suggested a fearful desperation, with his eyes sunken in from many weeks of worry. After getting into his office, Jim explained to me that right after he purchased the business the unscrupulous owner pulled the state bond which caused the TEA (Texas Education Agency) license needed to operate the school to be revoked. He then contacted all the existing student body and solicited them for a new school that he had started. Jim, the new owner, was left with an empty shell and lost over $100,000 in this fateful decision. Jim was a CPA, able to vet this project and understood the financials far better than I could, yet he fell right into the trap. He was asking me if I would partner with him to try to save the business. I expressed my deep regret for his circumstances yet told him I was not interested in getting involved. My gut instinct saved me a great deal of time and money. Now in this example, there were clues being given, "bread crumbs" that told me I should not do this deal. But how do we distinguish between experience and what we might call Intuition? Let's now take a few moments to examine some of the latest research on the Science of Intuition.

Intuition is often referred to as an "inner voice", "gut feeling" or "sixth sense". Depending on which experts you ask, the topic of intuition may evoke very different responses. Some psychologists would suggest that this thing we call "intuition", is nothing more than a guess. But new research is finding ways to measure these responses, we can think of intuition differently if we call it a *Rapid Cognitive Response*.

Research has shown evidence that intuition can be used to make faster, more accurate and confident decisions based on findings published in the April 2016 issue of Journal of Psychology Sciences. Joel Pearson, associate professor of psychology at the University of New South Wales in Australia and lead author of the study, shows intuition indeed exists and can be measured. The researcher defined intuition as; "The influence of unconscious emotional information, such as an instinctual feeling or sensation."

In one test, they showed dots moving in specific directions and asked the observers to use their intuition to determine when the direction of the dots would change. The researchers then embedded images that would flash across the screen designed to elicit emotions. Some positive, and some negative. For example, the images to solicit positive emotions would be a puppy or a baby, the images to solicit negative emotions would be a snake or a gun. The important part of the study is, participants were not aware that they were being shown the negative or positive images because the images were flashed at a speed so fast the eye and conscious mind could not perceive it.

The results concluded that when participants were shown the positive, subliminal images they did better on the task. They were more accurate in determining which way the dots would move, they responded more quickly and reported being more confident in their decisions. The study concluded that information subconsciously perceived in the brain will help with decisions if that information holds some value beyond what people already know in their conscious mind.

I believe that intuition goes beyond some inexplicable power, or educated guess, the study above shows that people are able to perceive information in subliminal ways (non-obvious clues). Intuition is also like a muscle, the more we use it the stronger it becomes. Let me put this in a simple way. If all day you sat around and made random guesses as to what would happen and call it intuition, you would have limited success.

But if you study the subject over a period of time and you watch certain patterns that become predictable, you're able to exercise your intelligence to figure out what is important and what isn't. In the moment where you have a "gut instinct" about something, it is based on this analysis and so has a higher likelihood of accuracy.

Intuition could also be thought of as clear understanding of collective intelligence. As new information is adapted into the mainstream, it builds a foundational understanding that allows us to more accurately use our intuition.

For example, most mobile phones use APPs today. A few years ago, many people were not aware of an APP or what it was supposed to do. Once the understanding became more mainstream, phones are now more 'intuitive' than ever (they no longer come with complex owner's manuals), which means today they are easy for most people to understand and navigate. This approach evolved after many years of confusion and different approaches on how to use mobile devices. This is how, as a society, we make progress and continue evolving with our intuitive sense because we share a common understanding of the way things work.

One researcher, Theo Humphries, called it, "the power of disciplined intuition." He went on to say, "Do your legwork, use your brain, share logical arguments, and I'll trust and respect your intuitive powers. But if you merely sit in your hammock and ask me to trust your intuition, I'll quickly be out the door without saying goodbye."

Thus, we can conclude from these different findings that; we should learn how to trust our gut, but make a concerted effort to continue to strengthen our intuition by doing research and becoming generalists in many topics. In my experience with the Modeling school, it was a combination of the things I observed about the owner's behavior and the "feeling" I had that something just wasn't right. In the end, my intuition served me well.

Albert Einstein said, "The intuitive mind is a sacred gift and the rational mind is a faithful servant. We have created a society that honors the servant and has forgotten the gift."

The Hidden Power of Voice Tone

We have already had a discussion in the previous chapter about the importance and power of voice inflection including: voice tone, pausing, emphasis, and emotion. But we can also use voice tones to affect our listeners in a more subtle way. Radio personalities and master of ceremonies (MC's) are generally preferred to have a pleasing tone of voice. Voice and resonance can create excitement, enthusiasm, or calm, soothe and relieve stress. To bring this in sharper focus, think about a professional auctioneer. They speak quickly and with a high pitch that creates a sense of urgency and prompts their audience to bid on items being auctioned.

Now in contrast, think about a late-night DJ on the radio; normally this is a smooth, relaxed voice that helps listeners to calm down and settle in for the evening. These two voices are very distinct, and as a *Ninja Communicator* you want to practice using different tones to affect your listeners emotions. When creating a sense of urgency, speak faster with a slightly higher pitch, use emphatic gestures that send nonverbal signals that individuals must act quickly. To convey authority, drop your voice an octave or two, and speak more slowly and emphatically. Also important in conveying authority is eye dominance, meaning you must hold your eye-to-eye gaze for a few seconds longer to drive home your point. Now many people will adapt some of these behaviors subconsciously, but a *Ninja Communicator* must be very intentional in these actions. It's also noteworthy to mention that while you are speaking you focus your intention on *how* you want to affect your audience. This intentional communication magnifies the way your audience receives your message, and the affect it ultimately has on them.

If you want your audience to laugh, take a note from professional comedians, when they want to introduce a funny premise they will often interject a giggle or two themselves which activates the listeners *Mirror Neuron*. Once the audience has been queued, and you hit them with the punchline, it's going to land right on their funny bone, exactly where you aimed it.

On the other hand, if you want to evoke sadness, then slow your pace and speak as if you are trying to maintain your own composure, if you can create a slight crack in your voice, this too can be very powerful. It will take a little practice because it involves some acting, but when done well it can draw tears from your listeners and connect their emotions to your cause more powerfully than anything else. Of course, you want to make sure that the narrative is moving and convincing when using this technique. Your voice can exude tremendous power when you practice delivery of your narrative. Remember, the power of the *Mirror Neuron* is often at work when an audience listens to a speaker. *Ninja Communicators* use this device to influence their audiences with deadly accuracy.

Some readers may feel like this is wrong because you are manipulating the audience. It's important to understand it is not our intention to use these methods to hurt or harm any individual or group. The word *manipulation* is often characterized with negative connotations, but it is not necessarily a bad thing. Manipulation is defined as *the skillful handling, controlling, or using of something or someone.* Our communication with others will generally take one of two forms; *relational*, or *transactional*, let's define these a little further:

Relational - involves developing a rapport, creating a connection, and having a sense of contact that often involves reciprocity. This form of communication may also be ongoing. Your tone of voice when being "relational" is generally warm, friendly and jovial.

Transactional - seeks a specific measurable outcome, sometimes involves an exchange with something of value like currency, it seeks a specific outcome and can also involve punishment or reward. The tone here is more direct and serious.

Whether your communication endeavors are to create a *relationship*, or a *transaction*, you're still looking for a *specific outcome* and as such you will use your power to *influence* or *create* that outcome. How you use your voice tone, will influence your listener and help to determine the outcome.

> "The face is the mirror of the mind, and eyes without speaking confess the secrets of the heart."
>
> St. Jerome

The Power of Eye Contact

Eye contact is a very important part of communication. When we communicate with an audience or an individual looking into their eyes gives us feedback as to how they are receiving our message. As a general rule, eye contact should be observed with other body language to be accurately interpreted. If their head is nodding, the posture is leaning towards the speaker; they are in agreement. On the other hand, if the arms are folded, the feet are pointing to the door, we may quickly need to change how we are communicating to reengage our listener. We must look not only into the eyes, but also the rest of the body language to get a clear interpretation of how our listener is feeling about our message.

Many studies have been done on what's called *Eye Dominance*. This relates to the amount of time individuals communicating spend staring into each other's eyes directly.

Depending on the context this can mean very different things. For example, two lovers gazing into each other's eyes, or a mother looking into the eyes of her young child, creates a deep bonding with the person's lover, or the young child. On the other hand, if a supervisor is chastising an employee or a police officer is questioning a possible suspect, this eye dominance means something entirely different.

For these reasons, it is important to better understand the role that eye contact plays in communication. All of us are familiar with having a dominant hand, being right-handed or left-handed. Most are not aware that a person can also be right or left eyed. To determine your dominant eye, try this simple test; look at an object on a wall and make a circle with your fingers with both eyes open stare directly through your fingers at that object. Now close one eye, then switch and close the other eye. When you closed your left or right eye, you should've noticed that the object jumped outside the circle. If the object moved when your right eye was closed, then your right eye is the dominant one; if the object seemed to move when your left eye was closed, then you have left eye dominance. Knowing this can be important for a few reasons.

When making direct eye contact with another person you need to become conscious of which eye you are staring into. Depending on whether you're *right eyed* or *left eyed* will often determine where you fix your gaze. In *Ninja Communication* this can mean something, so raising your awareness will be important as we develop our discussion.

Most of us by now are familiar with the theory of right brain versus left brain people. Recent science has debunked the theory that people are dominant on one side of the brain or the other. The facts show that we actually use both sides of our brain in concert to shape and form our views of the world.* But each side of the brain does perform some very specific function. For the sake of our discussion, let's identify some of those functions.

Right Brain

The right brain tends to be more creative and include functions such as:

- Facial recognition,
- Expression of emotion,
- Reading emotion,
- Intuition,
- Music,
- Color.

Left Brain

The left brain tends to be more effective at processing logical and analytical thinking such as:

- Language,
- Logic,
- Critical thinking,
- Numbers,
- Mathematics,
- Reasoning.

Right brain left brain theory originated in the work of Roger Sperry, who was awarded the Nobel Prize in 1981. This theory documented the above function of the right and left brain. Which eye should you focus on?

The actual answer to this question is; *it depends on the objective you are trying to accomplish*. As a basis for our discussion; it's important to understand that the wiring of the brain is crisscrossed, that is to say that the right lobe of the brain controls the left side of your body, and the left side of the brain controls the right side of the body. This is most apparent in stroke victims who may have a stroke on the left side of the brain and then experience paralysis on the right side of the body or vice versa.

Therefore, the left eye connects to the right side of the brain, and the right eye connects to the left side of the brain. When we want to affect someone's *emotional state,* we should focus our attention on the *left eye* which connects to the emotional side of the brain.

On the other hand, when we need to appeal to their analytical, logical or pragmatic side we focus our gaze on the right eye which will connect to the left brain. We determine where to focus our gaze by deciding which side of the brain we want to appeal to. Remember, right eye is logical and pragmatic, left eye is emotional and creative. Now this will take some practice, but it is a powerful tool in *Ninja Communication*.

As we focus on a particular eye, we must create a clear intention. Our *Intention* is transferred as we look deeply into the eye of the listener and continuously project that thought with our mind into the other person. It's important that we become very clear on what we want our listeners to think, and send that message nonverbally with eye to eye contact. Our attention should be placed on the eye and therefore the part of the brain that we want to influence. If this is your first time hearing this concept, you may be a bit skeptical; but we encourage you to try it, the results will amaze you. When you practice this powerful technique, and perfect it, you will be astounded at how the individuals you speak with will "mysteriously" adapt and accept your point of view.

There are other important aspects to eye contact. We've often heard it said that the eyes are the window to the soul, this is truer than many realize. Just as we may gaze into someone's eyes to influence their thinking when we speak, there is much that we can *discern* by looking closely into their eyes when they are speaking to see what *they are truly thinking*. When you want to see into a person's true intention it resides in the right side of the brain. This means you should peer into their *left eye* as they speak and this will reveal the private self. The public persona is projected by the left brain; this is the image that people *want* you to see, visible through the *right* eye. Their personal thoughts, feelings and emotions, however, can be seen when peering into their *left* eye.

Remember the brain crisscrosses, so right eye is left brain and right brain is left eye.

To get good at this, you will need a little practice. The best way to practice is by taking a look at photographs of people you know intimately; look closely at the left side of the face, particularly around the eye, you will see certain emotions portrayed; such as sadness, happiness, anger, or fear. This private person lurks inside of each of us regardless of what facial expression is being shown to the world. Once you develop the ability and know what to look for you will quickly and easily be able to discern the thoughts and innermost feelings of the people you deal with on a day-to-day basis.

Pupils of the Eye, a Powerful Tell

The size of a person's pupil can tell much about the way they are feeling towards you. There have been several studies conducted where identical pictures of a person were shown to subjects and they were asked to rate which one was more attractive. Consistently these subjects rated the image with the larger pupils as being more attractive, in fact in 90% of the cases they could not pinpoint *why* they made that decision. This fact has been known for thousands of years, dating back to the time of the Romans, there were drops that women would place in their eyes to dilate their pupils thus making them more attractive to their suitors. The fact that these earlier concoctions could cause blindness was an unfortunate side effect, but it does show the extent women were willing to go to be viewed as attractive. Larger pupils will generally indicate when someone likes you, and or is in agreement with what you are saying. Conversely, when a person's pupils are small, it indicates dislike or disagreement. A very important footnote here is that this *will not work* when out in direct sunlight, or in a very dimly lit room, *this is only applicable in natural indoor lighting*. Also, if someone is under the influence of drugs or alcohol, they may also display a dilated pupil so this tip is only effective under certain conditions.

> "The body says what words cannot."
>
> Martha Graham

Set the Tone through Body Language

Now let's discuss Ninja Techniques in body language. When it comes to nonverbal communication, our body language communicates louder than our words. In an earlier section, we discussed the fact that body language is being communicated on a subconscious level. The people you meet with or talk to can detect your body language and have "gut" feelings about you that could be positive or negative and this "gut feeling" will be based on the subtle nuances of what your body is saying to them. So, it is important that you learn how to control what your body is saying, so you can give people the right subliminal impressions. With a little practice, you will begin to transmit signals that will influence your listeners and send the right nonverbal signals.

First Contact

To create a strong favorable impression when we first meet a person or even someone we have been acquainted with for a long time, one of the simplest yet most effective ways to let them know that we are happy to see them is with the *eyebrow flash*. We generally smile and shake hands or hug when we meet someone, but to add an additional dimension, *flash your eyebrows* when you smile. The way it works is you simply (flash the brow) raise your eyebrows for a quick half second when your eyes meet your intended acquaintance. This flash coupled with a warm smile and firm handshake or hug, depending on the situation, will create the groundwork for instant rapport.

Other nonverbal signals during that first meeting must be designed to let the person know that you care about them as a fellow human being. This would include small gestures such as allowing your guests to enter the door first (this varies in some other cultures so do your homework if you are abroad), offering a cup of coffee or water, inviting them cheerfully to make themselves comfortable. If you are in their home or personal environment, find something unique that you can compliment them on to create further connection. As you communicate and gesture, be sure to show opened palms. A key facet to showing openness is the exposure of open palms, a closed fist or pointed fingers tend to communicate a more aggressive posture.

When you sit down, try to create a barrier free zone. It has been shown that meetings from behind a desk tend to create a barrier, this can inhibit open communication. If you can sit without barriers directly with your guest, you will find it easier to build rapport. When I was in my corporate position, the desk was in front of me and people would have to sit on the other side facing me. This arrangement often created a level of intimidation, if that is your objective, to establish your authority; then this structure may work for you. Personally, as soon as I began running my own company, I got rid of the traditional desk and got an "L" shaped desk that went against the wall. Once the room opened up, and the décor was colorful and vibrant; my visitors always feel comfortable when they entered my office. This is due in part to the fact that I don't allow obstacles to be between me and my guests. This is true when you go out as well. If you are in a restaurant, casually remove any barriers on the table that stand between you and the person you're meeting with; such as menus, salt shakers, or promotional cards so that there is a clear path between you when you are speaking.

NINJA COMMUNICATIONS

When you first begin to communicate you can also use the *Mirror Technique*. The mirror technique works effectively as a nonverbal rapport builder, the way it works is you simply assume the posture and body language that your guest has taken on, as if you are *mirroring them exactly*. Once you begin speaking and engaging them, slowly begin to change your body language to show connection with them. If your prospect begins to mirror *your body language,* then you have won them over and they are susceptible to your suggestions and influence. When you couple this with direct intentional eye contact it can be a powerful tool in your Ninja Arsenal.

In addition, if you want to establish dominance you can create that with body language in a technique we call *power posing*. A universal sign of dominance, or alfa behavior, is to expand our body through posing. When someone shrinks through their body language by concave shoulders, arms pulled-in, and legs together, this is a sign of submission. A good way to put this in perspective is to look at the animal kingdom; think rooster or puffer fish; these animals inflate the size of their bodies to intimidate potential rivals. If, however we looked at a dog and he were intimidated or afraid, he sticks his tail between his legs and crouches in a low position, people unconsciously do the same thing. Interesting studies have been conducted by social scientist that show

how individuals that assume expanded body poses tend to increase testosterone, which is the dominance hormone and decrease cortisol, which is the stress hormone, just by assuming the pose it changes the level of hormones in the body.

These studies would suggest that if you are entering an intimidating situation such as; a job interview, meeting new people, or being placed in any situation where you must exude control, then holding shoulders back head erect and when sitting expand the body, you will communicate to those around you that you are confident and in control. Now you may be thinking, "yes but what if I am intimidated?"

That may very well be, but the advice here is; don't fake it 'til you make it, fake it 'til you *become it*! That's right, in time if you continue to display this confidence in your body language, you will begin to *own* that belief and *become* that person. In Neurolinguistic Programming, Power Posing is a technique that is often used to help change your state of mind by changing your body language.

Understanding Social Hierarchy

Nonverbal cues are occurring in real time constantly, you can think of them like sub-titles in a foreign film, explaining through body movement and micro-expressions what is really being said. For example, there is clearly a social hierarchy in most settings, particularly in a workplace where there are "vertical" layers of relationships, from superiors to subordinates. The boss shows power through their stance (power posture), how much they talk and the assertive tone they use, if they interrupt or listen politely, and command subservience with their gestures. Some research indicates that unfortunately, for women, some of these nonverbal cues can be misinterpreted. When we contrast this to men, women who show their higher power by talking more aggressively and authoritatively are negatively perceived by others, as are women who become visibly angry.

Today many women are in authority and the most effective way to overcome some of these social biases; is by first being aware of them, and second, conditioning subordinates to *your style* of communication and how you express your authority. Since gender roles have been part of the DNA of society for so long, let's take them into account. If you're a man, consider if displaying alpha behaviors can be interpreted as trying to overpower your female supervisor, and if you are a woman in charge, are you sending out subliminal signals of submissiveness to your subordinates?

These non-verbal signals could be a conflict for some that may not be aware that it is happening. I mentored a very smart young lady, who was a beautiful 30-year-old female.

Through her hard work and diligence, she was promoted to Field Supervisor in her company. Her subordinates consisted of predominately males in their 40s, who really didn't take her seriously. I don't know to what extent chauvinism was a factor here but for her it was an intimidating situation. She was being disrespected, her recommendations were being ignored, and she was miserable. When she approached me with the problem, I asked her to begin paying attention to the non-verbal signals around her. What did her body language say? How were they regarding her in her new role? Once she tuned in, she realized that she was not showing authority in her tone or posture, and that her subordinates picked up on this "subliminal" lack of confidence and disregarded her authority. She quickly began making changes, to her posture, her body language and her tone. When someone questioned her, she responded quickly with Eye Dominance, a firm tone and a clear, unambiguous message. Before long, all of them fell in line and the team's productivity increased. Again, words can be saying one thing but your body language can betray you if you are not aware of the messages you convey.

Now let's consider a few signs that may give us deeper insight on a person's inner thinking.

NINJA COMMUNICATIONS

"If you're playing a poker game and you look around the table and can't tell who the sucker is, it's you."

Paul Newman

Look for the *Tell*

We are all familiar with the childhood fable *Pinocchio*, every time he told a lie his nose would grow. There is more truth to this than many realize; if you are speaking to a group, watch your listeners while you speak. If during the conversation they scratch or rub their nose, there is a very strong possibility that they disagree with what is being said. As a speaker that's your cue to adjust your message or provide further proof to back up your statements.

In fact, even if *they* are speaking and they tell a lie, they may rub or scratch their nose. In poker, this would be known as *A Tell*. People will have different tells but nose scratching or rubbing is a common indicator of disagreement or insincerity. Of course, it's possible that the person's nose may actually just be itching, so it is important to look at the context of what they are saying or hearing *when* they rub or scratch their nose.

What if they have a different *Tell*? What if they have a different way they show this disagreement or deception? A professional polygraph technician is trained to observe what's called a "baseline". At the beginning of a polygraph test the technician asks certain questions that they know the answer to, this establishes a "baseline". They may ask "true or false; is your name John Smith?" Since this is a true statement, they are looking for an outcome that establishes the standard. Once they've determined this baseline, then it is easier to detect deception. We can do the same when speaking to someone. If there is a topic that is disagreeable to them, or they may hear a statement that they strongly disagree to, watch them very closely *at the very moment of these comments*.

It is very likely that the person will show their disagreement through specific facial expressions or body language in that moment. Take a mental note and watch for consistency of this sign, when you have seen it a few times in moments of disagreement, you now have your "tell". This can establish a baseline as you progress in the conversation. This technique will be easier to master with coworkers, family, or people you are around on a regular basis. If the person is a stranger to you, you will need to watch them very closely and look for signs as soon as you begin engaging them. It should go without saying that you never reveal what you are

NINJA COMMUNICATIONS

observing to anyone, in keeping with the traditions of a Ninja, your greatest weapon is stealth.

> "Gratitude is the healthiest of all human emotions. The more you express gratitude for what you have, the more likely you will have even more to express gratitude for."
>
> **Zig Ziglar**

• SECTION FIVE •

Emotions and the Cause-and-Effect on our Bodies

The Power of the Mind Over the Body

ONE OF THE MOST POWERFUL THINGS you will learn in this book is reading the body through Emotional Causation. How does the body communicate with itself? This communication is driven by emotion and takes the form of a person's *belief systems*. Beliefs are extremely powerful, so much so that it can and does affect our physical wellbeing. That's right, anytime someone believes something consistently enough, it begins to affect their health; if it's positive they can heal, if it's negative they can get sick. In some circles in the world of holistic medicine it is known as *Emotional Causation*. This is where a person's emotions and beliefs actually cause or contribute to diseases or discomfort in their bodies. Now before you dismiss this as some kind of new age mumbo-jumbo, consider the scenario we posed in an earlier chapter; you are in a good mood and suddenly you get a phone call that someone you know or love has been in a serious accident. What physical reactions would you have when you hear this news? You may feel nauseous, you may feel a cold sweat, you may feel faint or dizzy, you may feel weak in the knees. These physical symptoms were a direct result of words that came through the other end of a phone that affected your thoughts.

When your thoughts change, your body undergoes physical changes as well. If someone has persistent thoughts or a belief system, over time those thoughts will shape their physical health and can create disease in their body. If these same thoughts are positive and they have a disease, it can positively affect their health and they can be healed. Some well-known cancer centers recognize this, such as M.D. Anderson Cancer Center in Houston, they actually have a wing dedicated to "Laugh Therapy", where patients are encouraged to watch comedies and meditate on happy thoughts, and this works to improve health. So, I encourage you to keep an open mind as we develop this concept. I'd like you to think about people you know and some of the conditions we will talk about and see if you can find a correlation between their disease and their emotions.

It's an unfortunate truth that a lot of people have had tough childhoods; these experiences have affected their self-perception. Some suffer from self-hatred; they may secretly doubt that they are good enough. The most powerful disease forming thoughts are criticism, guilt, resentment, and anger. When these thoughts exist and persist in a person, it can most assuredly cause disease. Now it's important to mention before we discuss any further that there are several variables that cause disease: toxic environments, toxic foods, risky behaviors, certain strong genetic traits, and lifestyle choices. We recognize these and other factors can contribute to disease, but for the purpose of our discussion, let's focus on a few of the *emotions* that create some common problems we hear about on a daily basis.

Let's start by giving some minor examples of conditions that you hear about on a daily basis, consider the circumstances and the emotions behind them. When you understand emotional causations, and adjust how you interact with the person in front of you, this can be a very powerful tool in your arsenal to influence that person. Now let's consider some examples:

- *A coworker comes in and tells you they have a stiff neck.*

You may both conclude that they just "slept the wrong way" last night. In actuality, the neck represents flexibility, a stiff neck may mean that they refuse to see someone else's point of view and that they were stubborn and inflexible in their thinking.

- *Your parent suddenly develops a pain in their hip.*
  A hip problem could represent a fear of going forward in a major decision, or feeling there's nothing to move forward to.
- *Your brother complains of a lower back problem.*
  The lower back indicates fear of money or a lack of financial support.
- *Your wife or husband suddenly develops sinus problems.*
  This could indicate that someone close to them is irritating them, and they are denying their own power.
- *A coworker suddenly develops laryngitis.*
  This could represent a fear of speaking up, or resentment towards authority, so mad they can't speak.
- *Your boss tells you he's having stomach problems.*
  This indicates fear of the new, the inability to assimilate new ideas or circumstances.
- *Your best friend complains about teeth problems.*
  This indicates indecisiveness, the inability to break down ideas or make decisions.

This is only a partial list of common health issues that a person faces and the emotions that may be behind it. By gaining insight on the emotional causation of these problems, you can adjust your communication to connect with that person, selecting the right words based on *understanding their emotions*, is as close to reading their mind as you can get. They will be astounded at your insight and your compassion as a connector when you say the *right words* to allay their fears or insecurities.

What if they have a more serious health issue? It is important to note that these emotional causations are not always 100% accurate. It is very important to be delicate and diplomatic as those who develop serious disease will be very fearful and defensive. Let's look at a few examples of more serious diseases and what they can tell you about the person who's been diagnosed.

- *Your brother-in-law confides in you that he's been diagnosed with diabetes.*
  This could indicate a longing for what might have been, a need to control, and a feeling that the sweetness or best part of life is now behind him.
- *Your coworker has a heart attack.*
  The heart represents the center of love, this person could be lacking joy, hardening their heart, and believing that life is a stress and strain filled process.
- *You find out your aunt has cancer.*
  This represents deep hurt, long-lasting resentment and holding on to resentment and hatreds.

- *Your best friend is diagnosed with thyroid issues.*
  This represents humiliation, "I never get to do what I want to do, when is it going to be my turn?"
- *A coworker has a lifelong struggle with being overweight.*
  This could represent fear, a need for protection, running away from feelings, insecurity, and self-rejection.

Once again it is important to reiterate that these are not absolutes, but can be used as a guideline to give insight to a person's emotional state. There are books written on the subject if you would like to delve deeper and gain a greater understanding to the mind-body connection. One of the foremost authorities in this area is an author and spiritual leader by the name of, Louise Hay in a book she wrote titled *You Can Heal Your Life.* Studying this topic will not only give insight on others and their diseases, but more importantly will help you to better understand yourself. It will help you recognize some of the physical health challenges you may be dealing with and how you can change these patterns, and change your life.

Personally, as a Ninja Communicator, I have used these techniques many times in building a true connection with people I meet. For instance, I had a meeting with a very wealthy client who I was interested in doing business with.

When the man entered my office, I noticed what appeared to be a medical scar on his neck. I positioned the conversation for a moment around health and he told me he had a thyroid problem and needed to have surgery. I immediately connected the dots, remember a thyroid problem means that for a long time this man's been thinking; *"I never get to do what I want to do, when is it going to be my turn?"* So, in my conversation with him I said, "You know John, we often spend an entire lifetime serving others, and while that's a really noble thing to do, we get to a time where we have to ask ourselves, when do I get to follow my passion and do the things that truly bring me joy?" When I said these words, I watched his body language shift; to him it was as if I had read his mind. He thought for a moment and then he confides in me; "You know it's so funny that you say that because I have been feeling that way for a long time." I nodded compassionately and gently said, "We are at an age where we *have to seize the now*." He agreed wholeheartedly and decided to do business with me because of the way I connected.

This can also work to improve your personal relationships. In one instance, I had been in a long-term relationship and my girlfriend and I had a disagreement. The next morning when she woke up, she complained of a stiff neck on her *right side*. Now you may recall; a stiff neck may mean *that the person refuses to see someone else's point of view and that they are being stubborn and inflexible in their thinking.* Since the pain was on the *right side*, I know that this represents the problem was with a significant male in her life, which in this case was me. So, while she was trying to act like the disagreement was not that big of a deal, it had obviously affected her *emotionally and physically*. So, I offered to massage her neck and as I gently messaged her, I said, "You know sweetheart, I was thinking about our disagreement last night, and I am sorry I reacted that way, I do respect your point of view and while we may disagree it's important to respect each other's feelings." She deeply appreciated my words and within minutes, to her astonishment, her neck pain disappeared. Now was it because I'm just a good masseuse? Well, I would suggest to you that it was my words that helped her more than my hands. The shift in her emotion allowed her to release the tension in her neck.

It's important to note: The Right side of the body is the Masculine Side; the Left side of the body is the Feminine side. So, pay attention to which side the problem is occurring and this can tell you whether the person is having a problem with a male or female in their life.

Some of you reading these experiences might conclude that I manipulated the individuals in these examples. As a matter of personal ethics, I use these techniques to help and improve relationships both in business and personally. I avoid manipulation for selfish gain or nefarious reasons. I would strongly encourage anyone that is learning these techniques to use them for the benefit of everyone and not for selfish gain. This benevolent intention will increase your abilities over time and will communicate to the people around you that you are a strong relationship builder. The name *Ninja Communicator* is appropriate; I personally view it like a true martial artist. If a person learns how to fight and he goes around beating up everyone he meets, he is using his powers for evil and it will eventually catch up to him. If on the other hand, he only uses his ability to protect himself and the ones he loves, then he lives a life of nobility. I encourage you to use these skills to help those around you and avoid self-serving manipulation.

> "Bad humor is an evasion of reality; good humor is an acceptance of it."
>
> Malcolm Muggeridge

Humor the Ultimate Lubricant

Unquestionably, one of the most powerful rapport building tools in your arsenal is humor. Humor is the ultimate lubricant. It can get people to like you quickly, forgive you if you offend them, or put them at ease in an uncomfortable situation. It's very important however, that it be used appropriately. I have witnessed situations where humor was completely misapplied. I once hosted an event for Domestic Violence, and when I introduced the male speaker he decided to open with a joke. He says, "What do you tell a woman with two black eyes? Nothing!" Then he yells, "Because you already told her twice!" While he got one or two awkward chuckles, the majority of the audience obviously found this joke was in very bad taste, some found it downright offensive. He lost their trust, and never regained it, even though much of the rest of his presentation was credible. The best type of humor is self-deprecating; usually when you make fun of yourself, you don't go wrong.

A more common and effective humorous approach is over exaggeration, which takes a common idea and pushes it into the realm of the absurd. Unless you are naturally blessed as a comedian it is best to practice your comment and your delivery, making it seem spontaneous and laughing a bit yourself when you deliver the punchline. Once again if humor does not come naturally for you, be very careful about trying to be spontaneously humorous as it can backfire when you're in the wrong company.

What gives humor its power, is the innate desire that most people have to laugh. Earlier we spoke about the *mirror neuron;* laughter as a behavior is quickly imitated. You need look no further than a 1970s sitcom to hear the fake *laughter track* that was played *over and over* after the actor's punchlines, this made viewers laugh spontaneously. Even when jokes were not particularly funny people responded with laughter because the mirror neuron was being triggered.

Humor is a powerful rapport builder, when most women were asked what qualities are desirous in a man, the majority listed a sense of humor as one of their top priorities. The fact is that when someone laughs with you it is more difficult for them to disagree with you later. There is a tendency subconsciously to view you as an ally rather than an adversary. Simply put, when you gain affection, you gain loyalty.

One other point of caution is to avoid overkill. This could alienate your audience by taking the focus off of your core message, so be careful not to turn your talk into a standup comedy routine. A few well-placed jokes particularly early in your conversation will go a long way in building the proper relationship with your audience.

NINJA COMMUNICATIONS

Some people use sarcasm as a form of humor, this can work for you or against you depending on what you say and how you say it. Sarcasm, when it is mean spirited, particularly when aimed at someone defenseless to its onslaught, will not be viewed favorably. No one likes a bully, so avoid this at all cost. So when can sarcasm work in your favor? It can be used effectively to flirt with the opposite sex. Particularly from a man to a woman. Think of the Vince Vaughn character in the movie *Wedding Crashers,* he is a bit of a sarcastic bad boy, but it was attractive to the women he jousted with. Sarcasm when used correctly can denote a certain charisma. If you can fire off a few clever quips with the person you're talking to and get them laughing, you will increase your ability to influence them very quickly. Once again, the caution must go out if you don't naturally have some ability here stay away from it as it can backfire.

"A good head and a good heart are always a formidable combination."

Nelson Mandela

SECTION SIX

The Science and Mystery of Energy

WE HAVE ALREADY DISCUSSED how communication is taking place on many different levels. In this section we will delve into the Science to better understanding how this communication is taking place. But before we get into this subject, let me address a potential elephant in the room. After hundreds of conversations throughout the years, I've observed that most people fall into one of three categories when it comes to this discussion, each can be dogmatic in their beliefs. There are some who believe that anything that happens in the world must be substantiated by science, because science is reality. There is another group that based on their religious constructs, believe that God is controlling things and if it is unexplainable then it's demonic. The third group, referred to as New Age thinkers, believes that the psychic or metaphysical world, supersedes what we commonly refer to as Science or God. The truth lies somewhere in between each of these beliefs. Science is a set of laws that apply to a preset series of conditions, when the conditions change, the laws can be change. From a religious perspective, yes, there is a divine intelligence to the design of the universe and the laws that govern it. From a New Age prospective, there is much that we do not understand that defies conventional physics; this is what we call the metaphysical world. Let's take a few moments to better understand this interaction and how each of us are uniquely equipped to sense what is outside of our physical bodies.

The Power of Consciousness

In 1947 there was a conference in Belgium on quantum mechanics. The top physicists in the world gathered to discuss how the laws of physics interact with our physical universe. It involved the top minds of the day which included Albert Einstein, Eisenberg, Max Planck and others considered to be the greatest scientific minds of all time. During certain experiments something interesting happened; any time there was a conscious observer, that is to say a person administering the experiments, results became 'inconclusive'. This led to the realization that whenever a human was in the physical space of an experiment it had the potential to 'disrupt the results'.

M.I.T. Physicist Dr. Claude Swanson, many years later described this disruption as a "collapse in the wave function in quantum physics" or what we might call a 'bull in a china shop'. This meant that our consciousness has the power to affect the physical universe.

This information if it were revealed to the general public, and if regular people discovered the potential mind power that they possessed, it could threaten the control exercised by affluent leaders of modern society. In fact Professor Hans Eysenck, who died in 1997, wrote a letter stating that he believed that there was a giant conspiracy between more than 30 universities around the world to suppress information about the true power of the human mind. He further suggested that hundreds of the top scientists were complicit in silencing the truth about human consciousness.

Discoveries that Redefined How We Communicate

When it comes to the topic of human consciousness, some fascinating discoveries have been made.   Dr. Bruce Lipton, cellular biologists, discovered "self-receptors" in the 1980's, these self-receptors, were contained in the outer membranes of our cells, which acted as antenna "receiving signals" from all around us. This led to the amazing conclusion that; our identities are not within our biological bodies; but instead is transmitted through a Field of Energy that covers the entire Earth! Now before you dismiss this as being complete hypothesis, there was an experiment conducted in the 1990s by Dr. Baxter, of the Heart Math Institute, who took cells from a test subject, put those cells in a Petri dish and separated them and that person by more than 40 miles. They then measured the cells reactions while stimulating the subject over 40 miles away, the results were fascinating, the cellular reactions were identical in response to that of the individual that was being stimulated. This showed that as humans we are connected to an Energy Field that is transmitting signals at all times.

    A more relatable example might be the case where a mother knows that her child has been hurt or in trouble even though no communication has taken place. The child is part of the mother and father's DNA, so they share these "self-receptor" cells, which are connected through the Energetic Field, even though they are physically separated. I experienced this personally many years ago, when one day around mid-afternoon; I suddenly had a sickening feeling in my gut, the feeling lingered all day. I went to bed that night feeling fearful and ill at ease, even though everything in my life seemed fine at the time. The next morning I received a phone call from my older daughter's mother, who at the time was living in Florida, she informed me that around noon on the previous day, my then three-year-old daughter, had fallen into the pool and drowned. Fortunately, she was resuscitated and brought back to life without any permanent damage. I never forgot that experience because it was clear to me that day I had the sickening feeling, something was seriously wrong, although at the time I could not identify what it was.

The Brain, the Heart and the Energetic Field

So how do we know there's an Energetic Field around us that connects us to the Earth? This too has been proven through Science in two little-known experiments that took place at the beginning of the 1900s. There was a scientist by the name of Hans Berger who discovered that the brain has an energetic frequency, that frequency later came to be known as the Alpha Wave. As the years progressed, more precise instruments were developed. These instruments were able to measure those waves to show the average human measured exactly 7.83Hz. In 1951 in a completely unrelated study, a professor by the name of Otto Shumann of Germany, discovered that the earth also had a frequency, that frequency came to be known as the "Shumann Resonance". The astounding fact was that the Shumann Resonance measured the Earth at 7.83Hz the Precise Frequency of the human brain! An exact match, so is this by coincidence or intelligent design?

These matching frequencies not only show that we are connected to the Earth, but that we are all connected to each other. This ties in precisely with why each of us has the potential to be a Ninja Communicator. The fact is that we as humans are both a transmitter and a receiver unlike anything known in modern technology. Most scientific research credits the brain as being the central part of this complex communication system, new research however has discovered that the brain and heart are electronically hard wired together, and that the human heart plays an even greater role than was once thought in transmitting and receiving these signals. Researchers including Dr. Michael Chaiken, Cardiologist and The Heart Math Institute; have discovered extraordinary characteristics of the human heart. The heart produces electromagnetic frequencies that are actually 40 times higher than the brain. It is believed that the heart literally sends electronic impulses to every cell in the body and in effect binds these cells together energetically.

Right now as you read these words your heart is emitting a frequency that can be measured 360° around your body with an instrument called a Magnetometer capable of measuring your electro-magnetic wave patterns. Research indicates these frequencies can be measured between 4 feet to as much as 13 feet away from your body. We can even measure frequencies on a common voltage meter set on Millivolts. The meter can clearly show if someone is sick, for example with Cancer or Multiple Sclerosis, which would measure 7-9 millivolts, versus a healthy person at 30 -100 millivolts. The body is very much like an A.M. Radio, it must be fine-tuned to emit high vibrational frequencies that others can "receive". When you want to communicate positive energy as you enter a room your state of mind must reflect that positive mental attitude and gratitude. When you are positive others can sense what scientists call a "harmonic spectrum", all the frequencies are working together. If, on the other hand, you are angry or sad, the frequency is on the "incoherent spectrum" and when measured, looks jagged and irregular. We have Seven Energy Centers that are emitting different frequencies from our body, when we enter someone's space they can "perceive" us on a vibrational level and instantly sense "information" about us.

These vibrational frequencies are unique to each person just like a signature or fingerprint. Our "Spiritual Architecture" broadcasts who we are to other "vibrational creatures" that enter our space. This is the reason we are automatically attracted to some people while repelled by others. There are also people that make us feel 'smarter' or 'funnier' when we are around them. This is because Higher Centers are at work in our vibrational frequencies which are opened up as a result of vibratory matches. John Gray the author of "Men are from Mars, Women are from Venus", says that these frequencies can help define what we have come to know as "soulmates". This feeling takes hold when three or more energy channels are open simultaneously, two people begin to feel like they are a vibrational match. A Russian scientist, by the name of Konstantine Korotov in 2006 developed an instrument that could measure telepathic communication and showed how Bio-Photon Emissions could send love directly from one person's heart center to another. It traveled instantly at such a high frequency that it could penetrate any sub-atomic barrier. This may explain why we feel loving and nurturing energy from people we don't know.

These vibrational frequencies apply in other areas as well, as we referenced in a previous chapter, in the psychology of sports we often hear athletes speak of getting into the "Zone". At a quantum level, this thing we call the "zone" is our system reaching an ultra-focused state, and crystallizing our awareness in the present moment. When we become ultra-focused we are processing more bits of information per second. When some people have an accident or enter the "zone" they report that it appears as if time is slowing down, this is how the brain interprets this accelerated process of taking in more compressed information in a shorter slice of time. Some of us remember the movie The Matrix when the main character Neo gets into certain situations and moves into "The Matrix", time appears to slow down and is compressed. When this happens in real life, this is what is meant by being more "quantum attuned."

Sensing the Future

Some Quantum Physicists believe that we can move 'in and out' of this vibrational plain and jump to other frequencies that parallel this reality; the two plains cannot "see" each other unless they are on the same vibrational wavelength. Some refer to it as the "String Theory". Recent research on the heart has discovered that the heart can emit such powerful frequencies it actually has the ability for pre-cognitive perception, that is to say, it could possibly help you predict the future. There was a study conducted by Dr. Roland McCrady where test subjects were wired to a brainwave monitor and a heart variability monitor. Each subject was asked to press a button. Each time the button was pressed there was a delay and then a picture would appear on the monitor, the image was randomly selected by the computer. Some were beautiful and others were horrific images; amazingly, the physical body of the test group, responded six seconds before the image appeared on the screen! The studies showed that the heart responded before the brain could see the image. So this thing we call intuition, can be gauged by how our body is receiving information from energy frequencies all around us.

In other instances it may not be about intuition it may be about what we've come to call psychic power. For those skeptics among us there is documented proof that has taken place in recent history. In 1978 President Jimmy Carter used two psychics to "Remote View" a location for a lost Russian T.U.-22 Bomber that had been missing for weeks and could not be located by any satellite or radar systems. The psychics were able to tune in and found the missing Bomber in a remote part of the African Jungle. Most people are not aware that between 1977 and 1981 Americans and Russians, spied on each other using psychics to "Remote View" each other's top secret installations, this 'Secret Psychic Spy Program' was later made public. One notable psychic by the name of Pat Price was able to 'see' inside a Russian building and he learned the Russians were making Secret Weapons that could affect the American arsenal. In reaction to this the next president, Ronald Reagan, initiated what came to be known as "The Star Wars" program.

Increasing Your Vibratory Signature

So at this point some of you may ask the question; 'How do I dial into this energy and enhance my frequency so that I am broadcasting with a stronger signal?' That's a great question, so let's cover a few helpful suggestions. Raising vibrational frequency starts with becoming more self-aware. Remember your body acts like a transmitter and receiver so taking care of your body is a critical part of this equation. Start a Regiment of meditation and deep breathing, there are many instructional videos on Yoga, Tai Chi and Chi Gong. As you engage in these practices you will learn the discipline of centering your energy. You should also go to YouTube and look up Binaural Beats, these are specific sound frequencies that help you to tune your mind and body. It is also important to adjust your diet, work on eliminating the excessive use of; sugary foods; animal products including meat, poultry and dairy, excessive alcohol, drugs and tobacco. These foods have very low vibrational frequencies and that is the reason they affect health adversely. Plant base foods pull their energy from the sun and have a much higher vibrational frequency so as you eat them you will benefit from this natural energy infusion. It is also important to drink plenty of clean healthy water; in the body water operates as a conductor that assists in moving energy throughout the organism.

The other work that is crucial is changing the mental disposition. In previous chapters we have spoken about the importance of your self-talk, what do you believe to be true about yourself? Another important step is to practice acts of kindness; you will find that by giving, you automatically raise your vibrational frequency. Practice gratitude, meditating on how grateful you are will shift your vibrational frequency in a way that others can sense. I would encourage you to create an audio recording or a series of recordings in your own voice where you state your affirmations, and the things you're grateful for. Make it a practice to listen to these on a daily basis and it will begin to shift your energy and your life. Finally it is important to get your blood moving through cardiovascular exercise which will also improve your lymphatic system and endocrine systems these work directly with your heart. Remember the heart is the organ that emits this energy you want to increase, by taking care of it, it will increase not only your vibrational frequency, but your life.

> *"Speakers who talk about what life has taught them never fail to keep the attention of their audiences."*
>
> ## Dale Carnegie

• SECTION SEVEN •

Public Speaking

IN THIS SECTION, we will talk specifically about public speaking. We've heard it said that many people would rather jump out of an airplane than stand in front of an audience to deliver a speech. The truth is, public speaking should not be feared, but mastered. With a few simple techniques, you can become quite effective at delivering your message.

A good speech should be viewed like a painting; first you create the framework, then you begin to add color, depth, and dimension. Once the painting is complete, you display it. When you look at the basic outline, it consists of three distinct areas:

1) Open – *tell them* what you will speak about.
2) Presentation – *tell them* what you're going to *tell them.*
3) Close – *tell them* what you *told them.*

So, let's address first things first, that is the fear that most people have of speaking publicly. The first question to ask is, what's the worst thing that can happen? We know that you won't drop dead, so the worst thing that can happen is making a fool out of ourselves. Now while this may not feel good, it does pass. When we think about the fear of public speaking, it is sometimes helpful to try to reflect on our earliest childhood memories of public speaking. If we were embarrassed or humiliated when we were younger we could still be carrying those memories which affect our performance every time we are put in a public speaking situation. Since many people fear embarrassment; the simplest way to avoid this is to prepare a solid outline and practice, practice, practice. Everyone has butterflies; the key is to get them to fly in formation. So, let's discuss the constructs of an effective presentation:

Any track star will tell you that the key to a good race is how you get out of the blocks. The same can be said about a good public talk, your opening is key to set the precedent for your talk. You want to be sure to begin with enthusiasm and confidence, even if you're scared to death don't let them see you sweat. Many of us have sat in audiences where a speaker was visibly nervous, clearing their throat, and fidgeting. How did that make you feel as an audience member? For most of us, a nervous speaker simply makes us uncomfortable. In most cases, your audience is rooting for you to do well. Start out with a well-rehearsed story that you can tell that ties into your talk, or if appropriate a bit of humor that builds rapport with your audience.

There are also effective techniques to gain control over your audience; one of the ones that I have used for years is asking a rhetorical question like; "true or false, knowledge is power?" I then look to the audience to answer, and when they do, I confidently *disagree* with them, by saying, "**False**, knowledge is *not* power; it is *the use of knowledge* that is power." Then, I'll challenge them to take the information I am sharing that day, and encourage them to *put it to use*. An opening like this sends a direct message to the audience, that you are confident and in control and what you have to say is important. You can also use a famous quotation and tie that into the body of your conversation.

Another important step in controlling the butterflies is to do a visualization of your talk. So, you rehearse by standing in front of a podium preferably with a mirror in front of you and deliver your speech from start to finish, pretending that your audience is before you. When doing the visualization; rehearse your hand gestures, your voice inflection, and even where you will be looking in the audience as you make key points. Some novice speakers have nervous idiosyncrasies;

like fixing their gaze on the same few people in one spot of the audience, rather than confidently moving their gaze back and forth. Additionally, be sure to work on the emotional intensity as well as the conviction in your voice. This rehearsal and visualization should be done 5 to 7 times. Once you've practiced, send a clear message to your subconscious mind by using positive self-talk, and if any negative thoughts creep into your mind, immediately reject them as useless thoughts.

Stay in tune with your body language. Put yourself in *State*, what does that mean? In the study of neurolinguistic programming one of the most important aspects is to put yourself in a *specific state of mind*. For example, think of an instance when you were 100% confident. How did you walk, how did you move, what was your body language, what type of eye contact did you have? These and other factors contribute to how you are perceived. When you walk onto a stage, your body language is the very first communicator that you have. A confident, enthusiastic stride will send a signal to your audience that they are about to get a great presentation. It also signals you to deliver your very best. When you begin speaking, be sure to use hand gestures this will animate your talk and it will engage your audience. You may have noticed a nervous speaker who grips and holds the podium with white knuckles as if they are clinging on for dear life. Confident gestures tell your audience that you know your stuff and you want them engaged.

> "Enthusiasm will steady the heart and strengthen the will; it will give force to the thought and nerve to the hand until what was only a possibility becomes reality."

Orison Swett Marden

Enthusiasm, Like Boiling a Frog

Another important technique is building enthusiasm. I like to think of it like *boiling a frog*. Of course you're wondering, what the heck does that means. If you took a frog and put him in a tall pot filled with water, and you placed that pot on the stove and turned on the heat, that frog would sit at the bottom of that pot and boil to death. Why? Because he is amphibious and will try to adjust to the temperature of the water as it changes. If however, someone came along and hit the side of that pot with a spoon, the frog would get startled and immediately jump right out of the water, and save his own life. Now the point of this story is that when it comes to engaging an audience, you must slowly turn up the heat, so you don't lose them, like the frog jumping out of the pot. As you build the framework in your talk, adding key points, creating depth and dimension, slowly crank up your enthusiasm until you build to a crescendo. This allows your audience to take the journey with you, which in turn will inspire and motivate your audience to *act on your message*. It is important to remember that enthusiasm is contagious. As you get excited, your audience will accompany you on that journey. Accomplished speakers understand that they can get the audience to mirror their emotions and in so doing, believe and buy into their message.

Proper Use of Notes

Another common mistake of novice speakers is being tied to their notes. It is best to use an outline, and highlight a few of the key points. The most important thing to remember is that your audience has no idea what you're going to say next. If you miss something or it is not stated the way you practiced it, don't let that trip you up. Remember, they won't know the difference unless you point it out. When mistakes are made continue to move forward confidently and don't look back unless you need to correct a misstatement that you have made. When you are speaking and you make a mistake, if you begin to think about it, it will cause you to make additional mistakes. In this case, you have to "get out of your own head" and stay focused on the core message you want your audience to receive. It is also important to maintain good eye contact, look for supportive faces in the audience to connect to, but don't just focus on one or two people for your entire talk. Be sure to shift your gaze from one side of the room to the other. If you choose to use a slide show presentation, be sure that the visuals are engaging and succinct. If there are too many words on a slide, you will lose your audience. A well-placed picture is far more powerful than a bunch of words.

> "If you go around being afraid, you're never going to enjoy life. You have only one chance, so you've got to have fun."
>
> ## Lindsey Vohn

Have Fun!

An important piece of advice here and it's one you might find difficult, but trust me if you can attain this state you are guaranteed to give a better talk: HAVE FUN! Yes, put yourself in a playful state of mind where you are simply having fun! There is an important reason for this. When it comes to public speaking most people take themselves way too seriously; the secret fear is that you will make a mistake and look foolish. When you're in a playful state and you make a mistake, so what, just keep going. The audience will forgive you unless you're so uptight you won't let it go. Of course, if you are speaking on a serious subject give it the dignity it deserves but in your head, don't take yourself too seriously.

One other important skill set in public speaking is the ability to read your audience. Watch how they react to certain things you say. Are they fidgeting? Are they focused? Do you see people taking notes? Are they laughing or appear engaged? These subtle indicators determine if you must shift your pitch, power, and pace. The best speakers keep their audience hanging on their every word. When you manipulate your voice through volume and pausing, you can create a sense of anticipation for what you will be saying next, thus keeping your audience engaged.

Public speaking like other skill sets, becomes easier with practice. Remember the old expression, "Do what you Fear Most and you Control Fear." Start with small audiences that will support you, such as a book club, or some other casual meeting. Continue to do it until you can build to larger audiences, then join a local Meetup Group that focuses on this skill, and before you know it, you will be confident and accomplished.

> "A leader is one who knows the way, goes the way, and shows the way."

John C. Maxwell

SECTION EIGHT

Effective Leaders Get Results

Effective Leaders Must Be Effective Communicators

UNQUESTIONABLY, TO BE AN EFFECTIVE LEADER you must be an effective communicator. For the purpose of this section, let's replace the word communicator with *connector*. To be an effective leader, you must be an effective *Connector*. When you connect with the people you lead, they recognize that you care about them as a person, and they will follow you to the ends of the earth. We've probably heard it a million times but it's worth saying again, "nobody cares how much you know until they know how much you care." A leader that connects creates a powerful sphere of influence;

subordinates will trust their supervisory opinions and judgments and will do their best to breathe life into his or her vision.

In this section, I will speak more directly to my personal experience, mainly because there are some important lessons to be gleaned in what I had to go through. When the economy took a nosedive in 2008, I decided that I needed to go back to corporate America to weather the storm. I connected with a Fortune 500 company and was hired as a sales representative. Although I had a history as a sales manager, I accepted the position to get my foot in the door. There were 20 other reps that worked in the same room with me day in and day out. Although I was cordial, I stayed focused on growing my sales. Each week during sales meetings I carefully chose my comments to reflect my appreciation for the company and my willingness to help my teammates to achieve their goals. It didn't take long for my directors to notice my positive attitude and strong work ethic. They requested I become mentor to some of the weaker representatives, a task I willingly accepted and worked towards the greater good of the team. During this experience, I was able to showcase my ability to connect with people and get results. As soon as an assistant manager position became available, I was the number one draft pick and got the job. This was to the chagrin of others with far more seniority, but frankly they lacked the skills of a true connector.

As an assistant manager and a trainer, I excelled. When the time was right and my director was up for promotion, I encouraged her to throw her hat in the ring and even coached her on what to say to impress the vice president for her to be promoted to the next level. This worked to my favor. When she was promoted, I was offered her position and became director. I had literally received two major promotions in 6 months, all due to my ability to connect with my coworkers. Now as captain of the ship, I was tasked with the responsibility of building a team of top producers. As many who've been in this position can testify, it is difficult to start as a peer and then become a supervisor, because not everyone wants to recognize your authority. As soon as my position as director was announced there was jealousy from those who had been there longer, and several groups who planned to sabotage my success to get me terminated from the position.

Simple Lesson from a Dollar Bill

As you can well imagine this was a frustrating position to be in. Suddenly, those veteran sales people around me began slacking off, being disrespectful, and influencing other reps in the rebellion. The very first step I took was sitting down with each representative and speaking to them privately about what motivated them, what their vision was and how I could support them. These one-on-one talks were valuable as they helped me to gain insight on how each person needed to be motivated. These meetings helped to deter some of the rebellion against me, but there were others that were determined to sabotage my success. That week in the Friday sales meeting, I asked each representative to take out a dollar bill, then I said the following: "Take a look at the back of the dollar bill that you are holding in your hands, what do you see?" Everyone responded, "An eagle." Then I said, "That's correct, now tell me what the eagle is holding?" Some commented, "He's holding arrows." Again I said, "That's correct, what is he holding in his right talon?" And they responded, "Looks like flowers." Then I took a moment and I paused and I said, "Actually, what the eagle is holding are laurel leaves. Laurel leaves represent peace, the arrows in his left talon represent war." Again, I pause for a moment for emphasis and then I asked this question, "Which way is the eagle facing?" To which they responded, "He's facing toward the laurel leaves." Then, I made my final comments regarding the exercise and looked at key individuals as I delivered the message, "Yes, the Eagle faces the laurel leaves because his first approach is to vie for peace, but he is very clear that if peace is not accepted, he's capable of waging war." By pausing again, the impact of my statement sunk in. While I am not a fan of management by intimidation, this method was necessary to establish authority, and to let the saboteurs know that their efforts would not be tolerated. Once my position was made clear, I kept facing the laurel leaves offering help, support, and understanding, with a clear directive that each of us have been hired with a mission to be the absolute best team that we can be.

As I conclude this story, I must mention that not everyone fell in line, there were a few terminations. Certain individuals refused to accept the new status quo and as such they faced the consequences of their actions. But the vast majority quickly accepted the challenge of becoming the absolute best team in our region. Within three months we began breaking every record that had previously been set, and for two straight years under my leadership, we became the number one team in the region. I was asked to train other directors on the methodology of building a winning team. During these trainings, the number one point that I made with my fellow managers was; *successful leaders must connect with their people and show them how much they care.* At the same time, I made it fun and celebrated the victories at every opportunity.

THE ART AND SCIENCE OF INFLUENCE

Praise in Public, Chastise in Private

As many supervisors know despite how positive you try to be, there will always be a few negative naysayers that try to spoil it for the rest of the team. My personal philosophy on this is to praise in public, chastise in private. I personally never liked criticizing anyone or belittling them in front of their peers. If I had to correct their course, I would do it one-on-one in a direct, but compassionate way. This approach garnered great respect and fostered trust within the team. Managers who make it a habit to berate their people in front of their peers will find this strategy to be short-lived, as resentment and hostility begin to derail the focus of the team.

Another key strategy to being an effective leader goes back to the old adage, "When the student is ready, the teacher will appear." As a leader, it is important not to armchair management but be willing to roll up your sleeves and get in the trenches and show your team how it's done. Introduce new and creative ways for them to do their job more effectively. Create a culture for open communication so that team members can make suggestions and recommendations to build success. This environment creates synergy and pushes teams towards excellence. Once you create this culture, some of your best strategies can come from your team because they are in the trenches each day and understand the job with more depth than the typical manager. If you implement some of the suggestions, it also builds their commitment and involvement in the process. Your team will have a commitment to succeed when you get their buy-in. As many great corporate leaders will agree, your greatest asset will always be the people that faithfully serve the company.

You Can't Send a Duck to Eagle School
Making the Right Hire

Top corporate trainers all agree that the key to corporate success is hiring good people and keeping them. This is perhaps even more important if you are a small business owner. The legendary John Maxwell coined a fabulous phrase, when he said, "You can't send a duck to Eagle school, if it looks like a duck and quacks like a duck, it's a duck!" Of course, some optimistic managers will think that they can bring someone on board that acts like a duck and turn them into a soaring eagle. While this may be possible, a question you must ask yourself as a manager is; do you have the luxury of time to change a person's fundamental disposition to make them something that they are not inclined to be? In the competitive corporate world, most managers don't have the luxury of spending endless hours training someone that does not have the fundamental prerequisites.

So, let's discuss some of the key elements to hiring the right people the first time. Finding individuals that are driven with *the right attitude is the key*. Even if you are hiring someone for a technical position although their technical knowledge is important; their attitude, approach to solving problems, and determination in the face of adversity, will shape their success or failure in that position. Will they take short cuts? Do what's easy, rather than what's right? Do they take ownership and follow through until problems are resolved? How can you as a hiring manager determine if a potential candidate has these qualities? Our next section will provide some conventional and unconventional techniques for making the right hire the first time.

Key Interview Techniques

To make the right hires the first time, you have to look past the resume. As a hiring manager, you will have more candidates than you have positions. As any corporate director knows the key is finding the right hire the first time. You will invest time and money when you make a hire if they are not the right fit, then meeting your numbers becomes a greater challenge. Here are some techniques that you can employ that although unconventional can help you zero in on the right candidates.

When a candidate shows up for the interview, before you ever meet with them, if possible, observe them when they don't know they're being watched. Take a look at their body language, are they alert and focused, are they nervous and uneasy? If possible, you may even have one of your existing, trusted staff members sit in the waiting area pretending they too, are there to interview. Your double agent can make certain comments or even ask certain questions and your candidate will have a totally different demeanor with your staff member. Their interactions with your double agent can offer you great insight into who they really are before the interview even begins.

Another technique I used successfully; is to set up group interviews of between 6 to 10 candidates at the same time. This can be particularly effective if you're hiring salespeople or others in very competitive positions. Once they were all comfortably seated in the conference room; I would walk in, introduce myself and tell them that due to the very large response of inquiries for the position this is the most time effective way to interview candidates. I would assure them that they would each get a one-on-one interview but first we will cover some general information as a group. I would then tell them about the company and shortly after that, I would ask each of them to tell me a little about themselves and their background in front of the group.

Watching this interaction gave me great insight on their social intelligence and people skills. I was observing everyone in the room, so I watched how they interacted within the group who showed signs of dominance, as well as how they listened while others spoke. These observations revealed much about their personality and dispositions. I looked at what their body language was saying; do they seem intimidated by the other candidates that were more qualified? Do I see a spark in certain people of competition or dominance to control the room? In these settings candidates assume they are only being observed when they speak, but in fact much more is being revealed about the participants.

These and other insights make group interviews a powerful tool when used correctly.

Once I concluded the group, I would tell them that if they felt the position wasn't a fit, they were welcome to leave. If on the other hand, they liked what they heard and believed they could be a valued team member, they should remain seated. I further explained that I would spend ten minutes with each candidate to decide who would be asked back for a second interview. Your company may already have two or three interview protocols in place; I strongly suggest seeing every candidate at least two to three times if you are interested. You will find that by the second or third interview they are more relaxed and therefore likely to show their true selves. Another important screening process is to always look at their social media page once you've done an interview. You will be surprised what some people will put on Facebook, Twitter or Instagram that reveals much about their true character.

When you interview them be sure to tune into their body language. Although it's natural for them to be nervous, notice some of the subtle *Tells* that they will show. Are they speaking confidently using natural gestures, or do they seem scripted and impersonal? When you are asking questions how good a listener are they? Be sure to ask open-ended questions such as; who, what, where, when, how, and why. It's best to ask questions, then follow-up to get them to support their response with examples of real life experiences. Watch them closely when they are recounting their real-world experience. See if it is a product of their imagination or an experience that they re-live as they convey the story. When a person speaks from their experiences, they animate in a different way. Watch their eyes closely. When a person is recalling an experience, their eyes will go up to one corner of the room for a few seconds as they access that memory.

Watch this pattern, if the eyes move to a different part of the room when recounting other experiences, look for the contrasts in the context of the stories. In other words, when they tell the truth they might look in one corner, when they are making up a lie they will look in another corner. Remember as we previously mentioned your establishing what their normal patterns are in behavior, then when that behavior changes you're looking for deception (The Tell). I also like to look at the way someone smiles. When they smile, do they engage the muscles around their eyes or is it just a smile around the mouth area? Eye engagement during a smile shows true sincerity.

In the second interview, if you are truly interested in the candidate, towards the end of the interview ask a few personal insight questions, such as:

- What's your favorite childhood memory?
- If you could change something about yourself, what would that be?
- How would your closest friends describe you?
- What was the greatest personal challenge you've ever had to overcome?
- How do you deal with rejection or criticism?

When asking these questions, you're not only tuning in to what the person says, but *how* they are saying it. Design a series of questions that require right brain answers. In other words, tap into their emotions and see how they process on that side of the brain. You want to discern if they are inherently a happy person, how they relate to others in stressful situations, and some of the core beliefs they have about themselves. Questions like these will give insight on how they will interact with the rest of your team and whether or not they will become an asset or liability.

Handwriting Can Tell Us a Lot About Our Candidates

If you can, practice having your candidates to handwrite a part of their preliminary application. The reason for this is to employ the science of graphology, better known as handwriting analysis. Although you do not need to be an expert, there are a few basics that can help in your assessment of candidates. For instance, which way does the handwriting lean?

- **Handwriting that leans to the right** - indicates a person who is generally an extrovert, outgoing, and relates to people comfortably and naturally.
- **Handwriting that leans to the left** - can indicate an introvert, the further it leans to the left the stronger the tendency of introversion. These individuals tend to work more comfortably by themselves or in small groups.
- **If the handwriting is vertical** - this is what's known as an omnivert, an independent personality that can be

a people person or can also be quite comfortable working by themselves.

If the handwriting is round and bubble like, then you're dealing with someone who may be narcissistic and a bit immature. It's also important to notice whether they dot their I's and cross their T's. Even though this sounds like an old cliché in the field of graphology, it tells us whether someone has a good memory or is forgetful. We also want to notice if the dot of their I's, are directly over the letter or does the dot appear one or two letters down from the I. If this is the case, then they will likely have a tendency to *rush* things and may not be detail oriented despite what they are saying in the interview.

When you provide the spaces for the person to hand write, don't put lines on the paper, instead see if they write in a straight line across the baseline or does the writing tend to show an inconsistent baseline? This will give insight as to their level of organization. Are they writing small or large? Shy is small, large is bold. What type of pressure are they applying to the pen strokes? These give insight as to their character? Are they frivolous in their spending? These and other secrets lie in their handwriting. We recommend that hiring managers take some time to research the basics of graphology; find some articles online, or a good book on the topic, this will give you a powerful tool to assess who is in front of you, without them ever knowing.

For those of you who may think this is a lot of trouble to go through when hiring a new candidate, my philosophy on this is quite simple. Getting a new hire put in place is kind of like a marriage; it's easy to make the hire, but much harder to get a divorce. Think about it, to get married you simply go down to the justice of the peace get a license and in a day or so you can be legally married, but if you have to divorce it's expensive, it's time-consuming, and often painful. In today's litigious society unless you have all the documentation in place, firing a candidate that's not a fit, not only opens the company to liability, but can be time-consuming, frustrating, and a de-motivator for the rest of the team. High turnover, never serves the corporation.

Depending on your team, you may also consider having one of your senior employees that has strong social intelligence skill sets interview your candidate as well. The dynamic in this interview will be different when the candidate talks to their peers, have them record the conversation on their cell phone. You will find that your candidate will have a more casual attitude and will reveal things to peers that they will not say to you. Also, if you have a trusted person they will ask questions related directly to the type of work you are hiring for, and this will give great insight as to whether or not your candidate is a fit.

> "The art of communication is the language of leadership."
>
> ## James Humes

Once You Make the Hire, It's Time to Strengthen Your Candidate

Once you have your new hire in place, now it's time to strengthen them and make them a contributing part of your team. The first step in training them well, is understanding their learning style; are they visual, are they linguistic, are they hands-on, or a combination? Understanding *how* they learn will help in the way you train. Another very important meeting to have is gaining an understanding of what truly motivates them. Is it job stability, or job advancement, is it financial rewards, or company recognition? These questions help you to understand how to keep them motivated as you build a relationship with them. Find out about their friends, their family and other things that are important to them. This connection will help them to feel that you care about them as a person. Remember, employees tend to ask three questions about you in the privacy of their minds:

1) Do you care about me as a person?
2) Can you help me achieve my goals with this company?
3) Can I trust you?

If employees feel confident in these three areas, you can create a relationship where they will follow you to the ends of the earth. The best leaders understand the importance of building *emotional capital* with their subordinates. Those who sit in their corner office, and never come out to connect with their people, will ultimately find their team will not achieve its maximum potential. They may also find that they have a revolving door; the strongest team is built on a seasoned staff.

It is also important when beginning the training process to help them to understand there are three phases to learning:

- Conscious incompetence - you know you don't know what you're doing.
- Conscious competence - you finally learn what to do and you're doing it well.

- Unconscious competence - you become so good you don't have to think about it anymore, you're on auto-pilot.

Once you create this clear blueprint, outline the specific areas of learning that they are expected to achieve, and a timeline for achieving these competencies. Most people will respond to timelines when the expectations are clearly laid out up front and enforced. People like structure, most will prefer that over chaos. Your company culture must reflect that from the outset.

Introducing Your Team to Your New Hire

If possible, introduce your new staff member at a meeting, give them the opportunity to introduce themselves publicly and tell a little about their background and why they are excited to join the team. It is also a smart strategy to express your public confidence in the new staff member in front of the rest of the team. This accomplishes several things. First, it bolsters the confidence of your new employee; second, it sends a message to your existing team that you are adding a valuable member that you expect will contribute to meeting the bottom line.

Psychologically, people tend to rise or sink to the expectations that we set for them. When you express public confidence, it sets an expectation that compels your new employee to rise to that level. When they inevitably make mistakes, you clearly identify the correct course and you reinforce the importance of learning from errors and not repeating them. Once again, it's important that you hire the right people that are determined to grow into the position. If you notice tendencies of laziness, lack of detail, apathy, or other traits that affect their performance, it's crucial to address it immediately before the mold hardens and it becomes a habit.

Your new hire will automatically gravitate to certain people on your team, it is best to make sure your team members understand the importance of keeping their communication with the new team member positive. If they are critical of the company, or company culture, they could begin sabotaging your new hire before the person is even indoctrinated to company policy and procedure. If you have staff support, sometimes it's best to allow them to be mentored and paired with one of your top producers. Your top producing rep must be fully equipped to provide a solid basis for training. It is best if you have the time to do the training yourself to ensure that they follow your protocol and expectations.

> "Leadership is about being a servant first."
>
> Allen West

Establish a Culture of Servant Leadership

Many managers are familiar with the concept of servant leadership; we have an obligation to serve those whom we lead. Creating the proper levels of trust and loyalty require that we show our people that we are there to help them achieve their goals. Perhaps we've heard the now popular quotation by Zig Zigler, "Help enough people get what they want, and they will help you to get what you want." This is a universal truth. Your staff will work harder for you if they know that you are on their side. To create the right environment, it's important that you gain an understanding of what's important to them; what are they motivated by, what support is needed in your department, what would help their productivity, what are their greatest challenges, and where are their greatest opportunities? As you help them answer these questions, you demonstrate the most important tenant of leadership, the willingness to serve.

When it comes to serving, some managers can move into a gray area that can compromise their position. It's important to distinguish your position as a supervisor and not a personal friend. When employees believe you are their friend, they lose respect for the authority of your office and will often take shortcuts, or not work as hard because they will stop believing that you will enforce consequences. In management, it is a balance between the carrot and the stick.

The key here is *balance*. View it as a scale, on one side you have their needs, on the other you have the needs of the corporation. In an ideal world, this is a symbiotic relationship. This scale will move back and forth. For example, let's say your new staff member is a hard-working employee that has given you 100%, and they come to you and say that their daughter is sick and they need to work from home for a week. If it is within your authority to grant this request, the scale has shown them to be trustworthy, so you give them what they need to feel supported in their position. If they have not built equity by serving the company and they are often asking for assistance in their personal life, the relationship may be more parasitic than it is symbiotic. At this point, as a manager you must make sure that they are held accountable for the commitments they have to the company objectives.

Building Productivity

Corporate cultures vary with regard to innovation. Some are very structured and system driven and there is no room for variation. This isn't necessarily a bad thing. For example, McDonald's is one of the most successful corporations in the world. They've devised a system where any 16-year-old, average high school student can run the front end of the restaurant. If someone wants a particular combo meal, the employee simply hits a button with a picture of that meal to charge the correct amount. All the foods come prepackaged so that preparation is minimal; the systems insure fast service and consistent taste of product no matter where you purchase it in the country or in the world.

There are other corporate cultures whose lifeblood is based on creativity and innovation. One of the fastest growing companies in the world is Google. One visit to their campus and it becomes clear that they have a very different corporate culture. There is a vitality and energy among employees where creativity and innovation is not only constantly encouraged but handsomely rewarded. This ingenuity driven environment fosters growth opportunities in a very dynamic environment that is in constant evolution.

Whether your company is structured and system driven or flexible and innovation-based, it is your job to encourage productivity and focus towards corporate objectives. To accomplish this, talk to the people that do the job every day, ask them questions such as, "What suggestions do you have that you believe would increase your productivity?" If they make good suggestions that do not violate company protocols, then it may be worth doing a beta test to determine if it can be implemented across the board. If the employees devise strategies, then you already have the buy-in and implementation is easier. In most corporate environments, there are usually two key dynamics:

- People
- Systems or processes

The manager's objective is to motivate people and manage processes. When people are motivated, they will implement processes with greater efficiency. One coffee company was asked, "What do they do to be so successful?" The corporate head responded, "We are not in the coffee business serving people, we are in the people business serving coffee." This corporate focus helped employees to remember that their most valuable asset is and always will be the people they served. Managers, particularly those in service related industries do well to remember and instill this corporate culture.

Presenteeism a Harbinger of Death to Corporations

Perhaps we've heard the term presenteeism before, but for the purpose of our discussion let's define it a little differently. We've all heard of *absenteeism*, which means an employee is frequently not at work, but presenteeism is the opposite. The employee is *there* but is not **there**. In other words, someone is sitting at their desk, but they are 100 miles away. They are daydreaming, surfing on Facebook or YouTube, talking to a personal friend on the phone, or any number of other things that prevent them from doing their job productively.

Every year corporations lose billions because employees are *there* but they're not **there**. So how do we counteract this insidious eroder of corporate productivity? The first step is making employees aware of it. Most people don't realize how unproductive they can be in the course of a day until they are made aware of it. Ask them to do a productivity clock, an honest evaluation of how many hours out of the eight that they spend at work on *actual company business*. Many of your staff will believe that they are productive 90% of their day, a more accurate number would probably be closer to 50%. Once you make them aware, then implement some fun ways that you can reward their focus and productivity. If their work is computer-based, your IT department may be able to track their productivity then you can do an audit and provide them with analytics on their productivity, the results will surprise them.

As part of this strategy try to implement ways that employees can take ownership. For example, you could do an exercise where you ask them to think like the CEO of the corporation, if they were in that position what advice or recommendations would they have for someone in *their* position? How would they increase productivity, save money, and increase quality? Exercises such as these can yield surprising results since those who are in the trenches, have great insight on the flaws that may exist in the current systems.

"Optimism is the faith that leads to achievement. Nothing can be done without hope and confidence."

Helen Keller

Cultivate Your Team and Strengthen Their Inner Game

When I did an honest assessment of my team, who at the time was performing mediocre at best, I asked myself what were they lacking? Through this assessment, I realize that many were not tuned in to what I like to call the *inner game*.

So, what is the inner game? Everyone has a voice inside their head, their self-talk, that is either cheering them on or leading them to doubt. Professional athletes are trained to understand that they must control these inner voices to reach their maximum potential. Employees are no different. If they are riddled with doubt, if they are experiencing personal problems or stress, if they are experiencing pain or health-related issues, they will not perform at their best in their position. As a leader and a connector, it is both your job and obligation to help them become aware of this. As you heighten their awareness, they will begin to tune in to the inner game.

The solution for my team came when I developed the *T.A.S. Force*. This was a product of my own imagination, I just felt like my team needed something different. T.A.S. stood for *Total Achievers Society*. I announced that there would be a new type of training available for all staff members; the rules were different. The training would be completely voluntary and unconventional; conducted in a more relaxed environment, we would help anyone who chose to participate, to tune in to their *inner game*. The excitement grew, and week after week more staff members came to the voluntary meetings. There we helped them understand their self-talk, their self-concept, how others perceive them, and how to create synergy to accomplish more in their professional and personal lives. The transformation in some staff members was nothing short of miraculous as some came back to meetings tearfully sharing their experiences of how they have improved communication with their spouse, their children, and family members. They also learned valuable strategies on how to resolve conflict, reduce stress, and recognize emotional responses to problems. These were valuable skill sets they were learning that expanded them personally, so that they could be more productive professionally.

As part of this training, employees were also encouraged to assess their health. Very few realize that when they come into work in the morning and they had a coffee and doughnut that was adversely affecting their productivity. Some began morning exercise regiments, others began their morning with a protein shake instead of the doughnut, and they were astounded at how their productivity began to improve, they had better mental clarity, and they made better health choices.

As the weeks went by, low and average performers started becoming *top producers*. With each victory, we celebrated and recognized each individual for their improvement. Morale increased substantially and people who previously did not get along, formed lifelong friendships. There was another change, which took place in me. I began looking forward to those meetings, challenging myself to bring high quality information, and I grew through the experience in a very personal way. As a manager, you will need to decide what will work best in your corporate structure. It is critical to understand that your most important function as a communicator is to be a *connector*. When you help people to *connect* to their inner selves, they will respond by giving you 100%.

> "If you know the enemy and know yourself you need not fear the results of a hundred battles."
>
> Sun Tzu

The Damage of a Fear Based Culture

Over the years I've worked in different corporate environments, some with positive supportive structures, and others with fear-based cultures. While it is true that fear is often the ultimate motivator, and that's why so many corporations and managers employ it as standard procedure, here are a few points to consider if you have the power to set the culture for your company.

When everyone is in constant fear of losing their jobs, they can begin to operate with a spirit of doubt. When people are doubtful, they second-guess themselves, they become defensive; they become territorial, and they breed a general spirit of antagonism and competitive rivalries.

The opposite of doubt is faith. When people have faith in their company, in their product, in their supervisors, they will work very hard to support that belief. This collective energy creates a synergy within a company that will move the company forward in the marketplace. When your entire team operates intentionally, this creates the law of attraction and your customers will *want* to do business with you. Recall earlier in one of our previous chapters we spoke of the mirror neuron, attitudes are infectious. If your team is infected with a positive attitude, it will transfer in the voice over the phone, the firm handshake or smile when they greet your customers, and the positive emails or other communications that they send out on a daily basis.

This will also be reflected in their overall attitude about life. Jeff Bezos, founder and CEO of Amazon says, "I find that when I am happy at work, I come home more energized and I'm a better husband and a better dad; when I'm happy at home, I come in and I'm a better boss and a better colleague. You can be out of work and have terrible work-life balance. Even though you have all the time in the world, you can just feel miserable and you would be draining energy. You have to find that harmony."*

Google is a great example, it has consistently been voted one of the best companies in the world to work for. Google's success can be attributed to this culture. Google has people whose sole job is to keep employees happy and maintain productivity. Each year, Google gets over 2.5 million applicants. That's equal to 6,849 per day, about 5 per minute! The culture attracts the best and brightest, the corporate headquarters looks like a big adult playground with in-house daycare, wide variety of foods, non-conventional work hours and a clear realization that happiness is equated to productivity.

This challenges all CEO's to look at the company culture they have created. Is it positive or negative? Negativity is just as infectious as enthusiasm. In fact, one might argue it is more infectious. We've often heard it said that for every 10 positive words of praise, it takes only one negative comment to erase the 10 positives. Another very important factor that may be attributable to health issues is a negative work environment. From a medical standpoint, when a person is under constant stress their body produces excessive adrenaline, if they live a sedentary lifestyle the hormone converts to cortisol, cortisol is an immune suppressant, in other words it prevents the immune system from working properly and the person is susceptible to everything from a cold to cancer. An effective leader needs to stay connected to their people even when the company is under stress. Showing compassion and empathy can prove to be a winning strategy. A manager that remains a *Connector* will build strong relationships and forge growth for their corporation.

The Art of Disciplining Employees

As many experienced managers know, even with the best efforts some employees are just not a fit for the position. When the time comes to terminate, it must be handled tactfully and compassionately. Some years ago, I had an employee who was not performing to company standards; I had to put her on probation which is the last step before termination. After I had the conversation with her, she paid me a very strange compliment; she said, "You are really an exceptional boss, you are an Iron fist cloaked with a velvet glove." I thought that was a very interesting comment, so I asked her what she meant by that. She continued, "You handle communication very diplomatically, you get your point across as smooth as velvet, but behind that velvet glove it's very clear that you have an iron fist, ready to enforce policy when necessary. I really respect that." This comment has stayed with me over the years and I've come to appreciate that handling people with dignity helps them to maintain respect and work hard to regain your trust. This particular employee did bounce back and she became a rock-solid member of our team for several years after that incident.

So here are some key rules when administering discipline:

- Never make it feel like a personal attack on the individual.
- Keep your emotions under control at all time, focus on company policy.
- Use the sandwich approach. Tell them what they're doing right first, then tell them what they need to improve, then re-iterate your confidence that they can get back on track.
- Be sure you have documentation in their file with dates and specifics that can be used, if necessary.

- If written discipline is required, tell them this should be kept confidential, you don't want them spreading their negativity with the rest of the team.
- Clearly spell out a performance improvement plan, make them aware of the time frame and consequences if they are unable to comply.
- If you must terminate, be sure you have approval from personnel department, and act swiftly, yet compassionately.
- If they are aware that termination is eminent, be sure to get your IT department to block their login and/or access to company email. This prevents them from mailing inflammatory information to any staff members.
- Have your assistant manager, security or you yourself accompany them to their desk to clear out their belongings and escort them from the building. Do this with dignity, but be sure you minimize potential for problems.

Termination of employees is sometimes a necessary part of leadership. A good communicator is proactive in preventing rumors and speculation from spreading. Rather than allowing a lot of speculation, in your next meeting do a brief eulogy for the person who's departed. Now while this may sound a bit facetious, it can have a positive effect. You can say something very simple like, "As many of you are aware, John is no longer with the company. John is a good person and many of you were close to him, but in some cases individuals are not a fit for a position. When that happens it's in the individual's best interest, and the company's best interest, that we part ways. As a team, we want to continue to encourage and support one another and meet the goals that we have set for this quarter."

If you've earned your team's trust they will respect the tactful manner and dignity that you afforded the individual that was terminated and it will also set a very healthy respect for your conviction to enforce performance standards.

There is much more to be said on management and leadership, in fact an entire book could easily be dedicated to just this topic. Our focus in this publication is to develop our communication skill sets as a leader. Remember some of the key points, leaders are *Connectors*; regularly assess your relatability to your staff. Touch them individually so they know you care. Be sure to hire well, so you're not forcing ducks to become eagles. Create a culture where staff is encouraged to grow in their position and personally as an individual. Recognize those who excel and encourage those who are lagging behind, keep a clear set of objectives in front of your team and manage towards those expectations.

"Trust is the glue of life. It's the most essential ingredient in effective communication. It's the foundational principle that holds all relationships."

Stephen Covey

… SECTION NINE …

The Importance of Communication in Building Relationships

Building Relationships

In an earlier chapter, we defined the two different types of interactions:

- Transactional
- Relational

As was mentioned, a transactional relationship is normally brief to the point and there is an exchange of value. Relational, involves building rapport with the person you are attempting to connect with. In this chapter, we will discuss the all-important ability to build relationships. We've often heard it said, "it's not what you know, it's who you know." This is a universal truth, people do business with people they like, and people they like often have relationships that have been forged through time and connection.

The Key to Building Rapport

I remember when I first moved to Texas after growing up in New York City. To say I went through a culture shock is an understatement. I remember when I first tried to conduct business, I would walk into someone's office or place of business and immediately tell them who I was and why I was there. Growing up in New York, I came from a culture where people on the East Coast want you to get right to the point. In the South, there is a different culture, it's considered impolite to simply walk in and tell someone what you want. Instead, I learned the hard way that it's better to have small talk, like a conversation about the weather or sports for five minutes before stating what you want as a way of building rapport. When it comes to developing relationships, the ability to build rapport is a critical factor.

When first meeting someone it is very important if you'd like to form a relationship with them to find common ground, look for points of mutual interest. When a person finds that you have something in common with them, they subconsciously view you as a person who is interesting, and like you. While we've often heard the term *opposites attract*, the truth is; *birds of a feather stick together*. So, if you can appear as *birds of a feather* with the person you intend to build a relationship with, they will be receptive to learning more about you and helping you to get what you want.

A key to rapport building is to show interest in the other person by asking questions. People like talking about themselves, and they like talking about things they know a lot about. This is referred to as *ego speak*. If someone knows a lot about exotic birds, they will find a way to engage you in a conversation about birds. Many of us who may not be big sports buffs, have at one point or another been cornered by a sports enthusiast who felt compelled to quote every statistic in the world book Encyclopedia while we stood helplessly by and passively agreed. While we want to avoid being put in this position, we want to ask a few well thought out questions to immediately start the process of building rapport. It's also a good idea to become a generalist. In other words, take a few moments each day to read up on a topic or two that you are not familiar with so that you can broaden your conversational acumen.

When possible and appropriate, it's also a good idea to create a humorous repartee'. As previously mentioned, humor serves like a lubricant to a relationship, when applied correctly it is an instant rapport builder. People like to laugh, that's why they are often attracted to comedians, or enjoy going to comedy clubs. No one wants to be around the person that takes themselves too seriously and does not have moments of levity. An ounce of humor is worth a pound of diplomacy.

Preserving Relationships

Whether with a business associate or a significant other, preserving relationships is the keys to success. To preserve and build a long-term relationship, you must build credibility with the other person. There are only a few ways that credibility can be built:

- Do what you say you're going to do and build a track record.
- Be introduced by a credible person that immediately establishes *your* credibility.
- Present a verifiable history that shows you are credible.

There are a few other ways but these three are core areas to being credible and building relationships. From the point of first contact with the person, you can begin developing a sustainable relationship by demonstrating small gestures that show you care about them as a person, little things go a long way. At the first meeting, simple things such as offering a chair to make them comfortable, taking their jacket or checking if the temperature in the room is comfortable for them, offering a glass of water, or coffee. These small gestures tell the person you care about them as a human being, and you can be trusted. Remember, people want to know a few key things before they build a relationship with you:

- Do you care about me as a human being?
- Can I trust you?
- Will you have my best interest in mind?

Once these core questions are answered, and you allow the person an opportunity to tell you a little about themselves, you are well on your way to forging a relationship that is sustainable. For sustainability, it is also very important to do what you say you're going to do. If for any reason you cannot honor a commitment, follow-up immediately with an apology and let the person know what you will do to either fulfill your promise or compensate them for your failure to honor your commitment. Another very effective strategy is to promulgate a culture of caring by remembering anniversaries, birthdays, and other special events. If someone is sick or someone they love is not well, or has passed away, be sure to show your sympathy or lend your condolences.

NINJA COMMUNICATIONS

On a few occasions, I have offered a kind word to someone going through challenges and it changed their lives unbeknownst to me. On one such occasion I met a guy we will call, Michael. Michael was always very complimentary of me and appeared to have a positive attitude. I didn't know him particularly well but one day he called me, said he was having a bad time, and I offered a few words of encouragement. For me, it was a small gesture that I forgot about. A year later, I ran into Michael and he told me I saved his life. I thought that was an exaggeration so I asked, "What do you mean 'I saved your life?'" He then tearfully confessed that when he called me, he was planning to commit suicide that day because his life had gone so wrong. Michael told me my words strengthened him, gave him hope and encouraged him not to give up. I remember that I almost didn't take that call. The lesson for me is; we cannot underestimate the power of an encouraging word.

"When men and women are able to respect and accept their differences then love has a chance to blossom."

John Gray

• SECTION TEN •

Men, Women, and the Chemistry of Attraction

WHEN IT COMES TO COMMUNICATION, most people will readily agree that getting along with the opposite sex is a big priority and can often be a big challenge. A loving relationship can give us great joy and a true sense of fulfillment. A miserable relationship can cause pain and for some, deep depression. Societal pressures seem to suggest that you can't truly be happy unless you're in a relationship. This, of course is not true, but many single people feel pressured to get into a relationship, even if they choose to be single.

The challenge with relationships is that men and women think and communicate in different ways. This is not just a matter of opinion; it's a matter of science. Let's take a few moments and examine the physical and scientific reasons men and women differ. Male and female brains process in very gender specific ways. While a man and woman may experience the same things at the very same time, it's possible that they will process that experience completely different from one another. Some of this has to do with the chemistry of the brain. For example, which hormones are dominant at the time? There are some powerful hormones at work, such as; *serotonin* - which helps regulate our emotional state, *testosterone* - controls our sex drive and levels of aggression, *estrogen* - a female growth and reproductive chemical; and *oxytocin* - often referred to as the love hormone, promotes bonding in relationships and is released with hugs and intimacy.

A man and woman not only have different amounts of these hormones in their bodies, but they also experience differences in how they process these chemicals. Males, high in testosterone tend to be restless, more physically impulsive and aggressive. We see these behaviors particularly in men taking steroids and in teenage boys that are producing testosterone at a high rate. Women tend to produce more of the bonding chemical oxytocin than men, which helps them bond with their new born child. This supports the fact that generally speaking, women tend to show more affection, particularly with children. While we don't want to paint this with too much of a broad brush, as in anything there are exceptions to the rule. Generally speaking, these tend to be true about each gender.

Another gender difference that has been the source of jokes for years is that women don't forget anything. Well, there is some science that supports why. Females often have a larger hippocampus, our human memory center. As a result, girls and women tend to absorb more sensory and emotional information than males. Women are able to use information from all five senses a little more efficiently. Men tend to have the ability to build and construct with less effort and use their spatial relations skills more effectively. While it's not my intent to stereotype, or cast judgments, the point of this discussion is to draw a very clear distinction between male and female brains.* With this basic understanding, let's now discuss some of the dynamics of male and female communications.

What about relationships with our significant other? Often when we are under stress, or depressed; we will strike out against the people closest to us. Our most important relationships are with the people we love. It's important to understand that when it comes to communication; men and women have different needs. As a general rule, a woman needs to feel loved and given attention. This sends a message that she is valued and honored as someone special in a man's life. Men on the other hand, need to feel trusted and respected; this makes them feel competent and assures their ego is satisfied. Understanding this subtle, but significant difference should change the way you communicate with the opposite gender. Within the relationship, it is important that each of you define what you need to feel fulfilled. Don't assume that your significant other knows those needs, be sure to communicate them clearly, and be sure that there is mutual understanding.

It is also very important not to trivialize what is important to your partner. If something is important to them, we strengthen our relationship when we regard that issue or matter as important to us. We must also use inclusive language; that is to say "we", "us" and other terms that communicate we are a team. When those words are used, it puts our partner at ease and helps them to view the relationship as an alliance rather than two separate camps. This language also works well in business when we are building teamwork into a framework.

Another important factor in an intimate relationship is recognizing the shift from the "honeymoon stage", to a sustainable relationship. During the first 3 to 6 months, most couples are enamored by each other and tend to overlook what will later become annoying habits or tendencies. Effectively communicating from the beginning will lessen the transition once the honeymoon has ended. One way to look at it, is that good communication and clever repartee' builds the foundation of connection. This helps in moving gracefully from honeymoon to a deeper, more meaningful relationship. Once this time has passed, your significant other needs to know that you are credible, and you will do what you say you're going to do and you can be trusted. Often, when a relationship fails it is because one or both partners have lost credibility in the eyes of the other, and so begins a slow separation and loss of interest. We avoid this by truly understanding what is important to the other person. When we honor those things, we build a strong, sustainable relationship.

The Chemistry of Attraction

Have you ever just gotten close to someone and felt an immediate attraction? We often believe that this is just physical, but a lot more could be going on beneath the surface. "Smell" is an inadequate description but it's often how we describe sensing someone's pheromones — a type of scent-bearing chemical secreted in sweat and other bodily fluids. Pheromones are known to be involved in sexual attraction in animals, and research suggests that they may also play a role for people. A type of pheromone called a *releaser*, which includes the compounds androstenone, androstadienone, and androstenol — may be involved in sexual attraction, according to an article published in the Huffington Post.*

Psychologist Bettina Pause, who conducted some extensive studies on pheromones, told *Scientific American,* "We've just started to understand that there is communication below the level of consciousness, my guess is that a lot of our communication is influenced by chemosignals."

These "chemosignals" influence our communication, why are we immediately flirtatious and playful with someone, while being serious and direct with someone else? How are the chemical signals affecting the male and female interactions? In one study, women were asked to smell men's sweaty undershirts. As unpleasant as this might sound, astoundingly the women were accurately able to identify the most attractive, virile men, just by their scents.

Similar research was also conducted at the University of Texas in Austin which investigated this phenomenon by asking a group of men to smell the T-shirts of women and assess which ones they found most pleasing. One portion of the women was asked to sleep in the t-shirts during ovulation, when they were most fertile. Overwhelmingly, the men judged the shirts worn by the fertile women to be more "pleasant" and "sexy". This led to the conclusion that a woman gives off a different scent which may make her more attractive to potential male suitors when she is most likely to reproduce. While we may not like the comparison, we have all seen the results of a cat or dog "in heat", they attract suitors from everywhere.

This teaches us that attraction is vastly more complex than just physical attraction to the opposite sex. There is an intricate communication taking place on a chemical level that we may not even be aware of unless we tune in to that dynamic. I recall my own experience with this. As a skilled salsa dancer, I have enjoyed going out and dancing as a form of exercise for years, and as many of my friends would tell you, I tend to sweat. On one occasion, I laughed out loud while dancing with an attractive lady from another country and apologized for getting my sweat on her. She responded, "No, I like your sweat, you're the only man here who's sweat I don't mind." This was funny to me, because she was dead serious. There was clearly a chemical compatibility between us that went beyond the physical attraction; we ended up dating for several years after that. So, when it comes to the opposite sex, pay attention to chemosignals, it could lead to the person you've been looking for.

A New Way to View the Experience of Communication

As we conclude our discussion, we should now view the art of communication as a "full contact sport". That is to say, that all five senses are involved, and our sixth sense is involved as well. When we receive a message from someone, we are "hearing" with our ears, eyes, nose, touch, and metaphysical senses. It is crucial as a *Ninja Communicator* that you engage *all of these senses* to receive or communicate the complete message.

Communication patterns are set early in life. What did we hear and see as children? Were our parents sarcastic, humorous, serious, argumentative, or angry? How did we filter these experiences? It is important to become aware of the fact that there is a complex and intricate pattern of words, smells, tastes, sights and sounds that have shaped our perceptions of the world. Every day when we interact with the people and messages that enter into our space, this complex network of thoughts is activated. That's why it becomes so important in how we spend our time and what we allow into our space. If we focus our attention on violence, fear or hateful things, this will download to our hard drive, and by default will infect our children and others we influence that enter our space. If on the other hand, we focus on love, positive and constructive messages we will grow in wisdom and spirituality. This isn't just some altruistic mumbo jumbo, there are instruments that can actually measure love and hate as emotions that translates to vibrational frequencies in the body; one heals, the other causes sickness. Each of us must make a personal decision as to which we will allow into our experience.

So, going forward when you connect with the people around you, it is my sincere hope that you will engage the experience with the new tools that you've acquired; that you are open to the deeper understanding of this intricate tapestry that we call communication.

A true Ninja practices over a lifetime to master their skills. I recommend that you read this book again several times with a highlighting pen in hand and practice the different communication and listening techniques until they become an engrained part of your thoughts and behavior. Learn how to convey messages intentionally, so that people are moved to do what you want them to do. Mastering these techniques will improve every aspect of your life. This is not an overstatement, it's a fact. Every part of your life is governed by communication, how you communicate with others and how you relate to self. Get this book and give it as a gift to the people you care about. Invite your friends and family to read and learn these techniques, it will foster better communication in your families, relationships and work places.

My life has personally been blessed because at an early age I became conscious of how to communicate effectively. It is my sincere hope that you will improve your relationships and enhance your quality of life as you move through the world as a *Ninja Communicator*.

References

Body Language and Nonverbal Communication – Page 39
Thompson Ph.D, Jeff, (September 30, 2011). "Is Nonverbal Communication a Numbers Game?" *Psychology Today*. Retrieved from https://www.psychologytoday.com/blog/beyond-words/201109/is-nonverbal-communication-numbers-game

Body Language and Nonverbal Communication – Page 40
Mlodinow, Leonard, (2012). "Subliminal: How Your Unconscious Mind Rules Your Behavior." Print edition; page 4.

The Power of Emotional Speech – 52
Levine, Michael, (July 12, 2012). "Delving into the logical and emotional sides of the human brain." *Psychology Today*. Retrieved from https://www.psychologytoday.com/blog/the-divided-mind/201207/logic-and-emotion

Listening an Active Process – 57
Adler, Ronald B., Rosenfeld, Lawerence B., Proctor, Russell F., (2001). "Interplay: The Process of Interpersonal Communication." Print edition.

The Secret of the Mirror Neuron – Page 74
Dapretto, M. Davies MS, Pfeifer JH, Scott AA, Sigman M, Bruckheimer SY, Iacobani M. (2006). "Understanding emotion in others mirror neuron dysfunction in children with autism spectrum disorders." *Nature Neuroscience*. Retrieved from https://www.nature.com/articles/nn1611

The Power of Eye Contact – Page 89
Nielsen, J. A., Zielinski B.A, Ferguson M. A., Lainhart, J.E & Anderson J.S., (August 14, 2013). "An evaluation of the left brain versus right brain hypothesis with resting state functional connectivity magnetic resonance imaging." Retrieved from http://journals.plos.org/plosone/article?id=10.1371/journal.pone.0071275

The Damage of a Fear Based Culture – Page 168
Soper, Taylor, (May 31, 2016). "Jeff Bezos says Amazon has the gold standard culture for innovation and pioneering work." *GeekWire*. Retrieved from https://www.geekwire.com/2016/jeff-bezos-says-amazon-gold-standard-culture-innovation-pioneering-work/

Men, Women, and the Chemistry of Attraction – Page 183
Jantz Ph.D., Gregory L. (February 27, 2014). "Brain Differences Between Genders." *Psychology Today*. Retrieved from https://www.psychologytoday.com/blog/hope-relationships/201402/brain-differences-between-genders

The Chemistry of Attraction – Page 186
Gregoire, Carolyn, (February 20, 2015). "The Strange Science of Sexual Attraction." *Huffington Post*. Retrieved from https://www.huffingtonpost.com/2015/02/14/science-of-attraction-_n_6661522.html

ABOUT THE AUTHOR

Oscar Hines was born in San Jose, Costa Rica and moved to New York when he was four years old where he grew up. He always had a keen interest in communication and human behavior, after a successful career in Corporate America; he pursued his passions as an entrepreneur. Today, Mr. Hines is an Interdisciplinary Communicator that uses several modalities to connect with others, including; Kinesiology, Graphology and Emotional Causation, when used together these disciplines allow for deeper interpersonal connectivity. He is a Certified Health and Wellness Consultant and has trained and practiced Energy Work and Healing.

Oscar is a Certified Professional Speaker through the Les Brown Institute and is host of The Synergy Radio Show, *Natural Nation Network*, a program that focuses on Emotional, Spiritual and Physical Health. He has appeared on local and syndicated radio talk shows for over two decades throughout the country, and has made TV appearances on local news programs including CBS, FOX, ABC and local cable TV networks. Oscar has always been passionate about communication and has skillfully interwoven seemingly unrelated sciences to produce one of the most comprehensive books on communication that's ever been written; **Ninja Communications: The Art and Science of Influence**, is a book that reveals the inside secrets to becoming a powerful influencer by understanding and using the *Science* of Communication.

Mr. Hines is a sought-after speaker and CEO of Synergy Broadcasting, a Houston based firm, which manages a Group of Radio stations and Digital Platforms including, *Synergy Radio*, *The Mind In Motion Networks* and *Genuine Journey*

Network which broadcasts independent conscious content on ROKU, Android and Amazon Fire TV. His mission is to help people gain a better understanding of others and self through enhanced communication.

Connect at:

www.oscarhines.com

www.genuinejourneymedia.com

www.ingramcontent.com/pod-product-compliance
Lightning Source LLC
Chambersburg PA
CBHW061310110426
42742CB00012BA/2129